The Nuts A[illegible] of Being Santa

Santa and the Business of Being Santa

Workbook Vol. 2, Edition 2

by

Santa Bertram "Gordon" Bailey, R.B.S

"If you can't dazzle them with your brilliance

Or bury them under your command of the subject,

Blind them with Bovine Excrement."

ISBN-13: 978-1547248148
ISBN-10: 1547248149

Published by **North Pole Publishing House**
in cooperation with

Fabled Santa – Santa Stephen Arnold
Fabled Santa Industries
1779 Kirby Pkwy #1-114
Memphis, TN 38138
SATBOBS@FabledSanta.com

Table of Contents

Foreword

This textbook "***Santa and the Nuts and Bolts of being Santa***" along with the first textbook "***Santa and the Business of Being Santa***" and the third volume "***Santa and the Performing Santa***" are textbooks used in the travelling Santa school known as "**Santa and the Business of Being Santa**". This is the Second Edition version that will be used in all classes from 2017 on.

The information contained will help you approach this business from the aspect of an "Independent Contractor Entertainer" and point out some of the most common problems and pitfalls new people to this form of self-employment run across.

The "Nuts and Bolts" will focus on the various people, businesses and manufacturers that support us in this job and give you many contact leads in that direction.

As with the first book, the information included here is dated the moment it was written but should give you an idea of where and how to further your search for new information.

Remember!

If you see hoof prints but do not see any horses,

Look for Zebras!

Dedication

I would like to dedicate this book to all the people and businesses that have supported this effort. First of all, I would like to thank the ladies!

- ❖ To Kitty Fisher who gave me my first real introduction to this business over 33 years ago, thank you for your never ending friendship and advice! May your voice and song ring through Heaven, until we meet again.
- ❖ Gina Bacon of Nationwide Santas for all of your efforts in making this School become a reality in 2014!
- ❖ Nedra Grice Odom of World Wide Photography for giving me the chance to experience being a Mall Santa in such depth!
- ❖ Judy Kidney of Dingey the Clown and Friends for placing me into so many home visits over the last 28 years!
- ❖ Linda Sutherland of The Fun Corner for supplying me with so many props and advice over the years!
- ❖ Sandee Gee of Full Spectrum Entertainment for such a long association ship centered around magic!
- ❖ Susen Mesco of Santa School Denver Colorado for all of the late night chats sharing information and advice!

- Carmen Tellez of Charm and Happy! For all the support and advice on the first book and your writings you allowed in the second!
- Rebecca Werner-Turner aka Curly the Clown for adopting me and making me a part of her family for so long!
- My niece Sondra Lavoie, one of the smartest and most caring people I know.
- And last, my sister Linda Pepper who has tried very hard throughout my life to keep me on track and centered.

To all the other ladies as well, thank you!

In the very back of this book you will find a special section that lists those businesses and people that supported this book and effort directly and I wanted to recognize them as well. Their contact information for the business is presented there in thanks for their support!

Introduction

The title of this text is "***Santa and the Nuts & Bolts of being Santa***" and the information contained was dated from the moment it was written. Since this is a companion text for the "***Santa and the Business of Being Santa***" traveling school, as new information comes available it will be made part of the lecture in class. You can update it with your notes just as with the first textbook titled "***Santa and the Business of being Santa***" and the third textbook, titled "***Santa and the Performing Santa***".

The SatBobS School began in 2014 and was held in Las Vegas, Indianapolis Indiana, Mesquite Texas, Highland and Ontario California. You might have a self- published copy of either book depending upon the class you attend or the timing of the publication. Eventually this textbook like the first will be available through Amazon and Amazon UK.

The purpose of this book is to help you find the Suits, Boots, Belts, Bells, Accessories, Educational opportunities, Employment Opportunities, and try to connect you with the Businesses and People that will support you as you do the Job of Portraying Santa Claus.

As this is intended to be a stand-alone text as well as a companion Text for the SatBobS school, there will be a small amount of cross over between the two textbooks in duplicate pages in the beginning.

Thank you for making the decision to read what I have to offer in the way of information and experience sharing.

Acknowledgements

I, Santa Gordon Bailey, wish to thank the following businesses for their continuing support in the creation and development of the Santa and the Business of being Santa schools concept. I am pleased to acknowledge and recommend these companies. Your patronage of these websites will in some small way, also thank them for assisting me.

ToysForSanta.com – Proudly owned and operated by *Fabled Santa*, Santa Stephen Arnold. This online store carries clever products, most designed by Fabled Santa specifically with the Santa community in mind. Please check out their Santa's pilot wings, wonderful reindeer buttons and other coat and clothing buttons, belts and buckles, brass bell sets, fashion pins, Santa key and a new Santa Global Pocket Watch – all manufactured to exacting specifications and using top quality materials and finishes.

NationwideSantas.com Owner/operator Gina Bacon provides employment opportunities to members of the Santa community throughout the United States and Canada. Nationwide Santas is a full service Santa Claus company, providing year-round entertainment to their clients. Join her organization and receive preferential rates on insurance, background checks and more. Membership is open to all who support the Santa community without discrimination – Real Beard, Designer Beard, Mrs. Claus, Elf and others.

NorthPolePublishingHouse.com – Charles Barnett, *The Servant Santa*, owns and operates this full-service publishing house, and offers assistance with graphics, editing and publishing, both in e-book and printed-cover formats as well as audio books. Working with Santa Stephen Arnold, Charles and Stephen have made these textbooks possible. Thanks Santa Charles for tying everyone's work together in these books.

Thank you to all who have assisted me with the ***Santa and the Business of Being Santa School*** and my series of workbooks. I must, however, extend a very special thank you to Santa Stephen (*Fabled Santa*), Santa Charles (*Servant Santa*) and Gina. Because each of you has so freely contributed your individual time and unique talents, you have helped make my dreams and goals come true! Thank you!

People that hire Santa Circa 2014

Hello Santa!
An over-the-Internet job opportunity for Santa that can be done from within their own home.

https://santa.hellosanta.com/home/applynow

Job Requirements

Must be an excellent Santa Claus portrayal artist!

Exude the spirit of Jolly St. Nick!

High-speed Internet connection

GREAT PAY

Earn up to $50/hour working from the comfort of your own home

WORK FROM HOME

Work from wherever you want, even the North Pole

FLEXIBLE SCHEDULE

You'll be able to choose a work schedule that works for you MAKE KIDS HAPPY

Make thousands of children smile ear to ear by spreading Christmas cheer

---

HireSanta.com

The Internet's Best Place to Find and Hire Santa!

Santa for Hire - Hire Santa has some of the best professional Santa Clauses in the world. These men are traditional holiday and Christmas entertainers that are serious about their appearance and presentation. **HireSanta.com** makes it easy for you to book Santa for you Christmas party, whether it is at your home or company; community event; or even mall.

If you are a GREAT Santa Claus and would like to be added to our database of Santa Clauses, please send: Name, phone number, email, website, picture and location to talent@hiresanta.com for consideration.

Noerr

The Noerr Programs Corporation provides turnkey digital event imaging and marketing services for hundreds of regional shopping centers, retailers and clients nationwide. We present The Santa Photo Experience and Bunny Photo Experience to 3.5 million family members each year at locations across the United States. The Noerr Programs mission is to deliver remarkable and memorable experiences to our guests through innovative marketing platforms. **www.noerrprograms.com**

Note: In 2016 the Noerr Company was purchased in a corporate merger with Cherry Hill.

World Wide Photo

World Wide Photo is another mall photo company that hires Santa to sit in a chair and pose for pictures. Like all photo companies they are in the business of selling those photos to the public.

If you are interested in working for WWP or World Wide Photo, Contact:
Becky Norman
Corporate Talent Consultant
Office: 281-547-6480, ext.: 4575
Cell: (281) 961-4988
Fax: (888) 205-0799

Becky is one of the nicest people to work with when getting a contract worked out. She will take the time to listen to your needs and then after the contract is in play, will do whatever it takes to deal with whatever problem you may have on or off the set. Their Saying is "Capturing hearts one smile at a time.

Note: WWP went through a corporate buy out in 2015. They have had some teething problems but seems like they are getting better at dealing with their Santas as of 2017.

A MAX Entertainment

We are a full service high-end entertainment company that can customize any type of entertainment to fit your needs. A-Max will make clients dreams come true and make their event stand out with lively energy, uniqueness, class and sophistication.

Contact Alysha Wheeler
@ (714) 726-1205
info@amaxentertainment.com

Nationwide Santas

Nationwide Santas offers Background Checks and Liability Insurance through my website. If you are interested navigate to my site and then go to the Santa Membership tab.

NATIONWIDE SANTAS MEMBERSHIP

Here are some of the benefits of becoming a member:

- Welcome package
- Nationwide Santas membership card
- Nationwide Santas Certificate
- Nationwide Santas Pen
- You will be added to our database and notified of job offers
- Insurance offered at competitive group rates.

Membership is available to anyone who supports the Santa community. Membership cards will reflect the type of membership:
Red Card – Real Bearded Santa
Green Card – Designer Bearded Santa
Silver Card – Mrs. Claus, Elves, etc.
Membership is $30.00 for 1 Year (Sep 1 - Sep 1)

www.nationwidesantas.com

Charm and Happy in California

Carmen@CharmandHappy.com
~ We bring the p"HAHA"rty to you! ~

562-237-332 cell or text
877-725-6967 office nationwide
www.CharmandHappy.com

The Kringle Group, LLC

Here are some of the web addresses and links for Tim's work on insurance and his other websites.

http://www.realsantas.com/liabilityinsurance.htm
http://blog.santahollywood.com/
http://www.RealSantas.com/backgroundc...//thekringlegroup.com/
School4Santas.com
www.getaheadstart.info
www.santaswardrobe.com
www.Summer-Santa.com
http://www.santahollywood.com/handylinks.htm

All of these links and much more are the work of Tim "Santa Hollywood" Connaghan and is a product of his hard work and love of all things Santa. Thank you Tim.

Tim Connaghan places Santas into mall photo situations, corporate events and home visits as well as facilitates overseas placement.

Santa Steve C. Whitakers

I'm looking for some Real Bearded Santas in Northern Calif. to help me cover several Events I have in Santa Rosa, Fremont, Santa Cruz, and Sacramento.

Please call me on my Sleigh Phone at 916-715-5224 or email me at santasteve.whitaker@gmail.com for further details, include three pictures of yourself. Steve places Santas into Bass Pro Shops, Malls and other venues.

Always Just for Fun Entertainment

Leslie Fulps Ramos

Hello everyone, my name is Leslie and I am an entertainment agent. I specialize in Children's party characters, Always Just for Fun Entertainment, **www.alwaysjustforfun.com** and during the holiday season I book real bearded Santas

www.homeofrealbeardedsantas.com

My jobs are mostly local, Southern California. I am currently looking for more Santas in the Santa Clarita, Ventura, Santa Barbara, and Calabasas area.

I have worked with and for Leslie for several years now and she is a delight to deal with. Always Just for Fun places Santas into corporate events and home visits all across Southern California.

Check out *Cherry Hill*

Cherry Hill Photo
www.cherryhillphoto.com

Welcome to Cherry Hill Photo Enterprises, Inc.

No one believes in Santa more than we do. Last year alone we placed more than 300 naturally bearded Santas in malls and department stores throughout the US and Canada.

Our Santas have even reached celebrity status, appearing on television programs such as CBS's "48 Hours," "Good Morning America," "Late Night with Conan O'Brien" and in advertisements around the world. It is easy to see why. Our selection process and intensive training assures that not only do our Santas look the part, they become the part. If you would like more information on how a "real" Santa can bring "real" success to your next Christmas photo promotion, please call Cherry Hill Photo (800) 969-2440 today.

Cherry Hill Photo Enterprises, Inc.
4 E. Stow Road Marlton, NJ 08053 / U.S.A.
PHONE: (800) 969-2440 / FAX: (856) 663-0880

Note: Cherry Hill and Noerr have been purchased in a corporate buy out and merged as of 2016.

American Events & Promotions Denver, Colorado

Contact us today! 303-665-8280

Book one of our many top-rated, experienced, Professional Santas to attend, entertain at, host, emcee and add FUN to your holiday gathering!

Private Home / Family Visits / Corporate Parties Santa Claus for Motion Picture Film work / Pet Photos / Photos with Santa (Great Traffic Builder or Fundraiser!)

http://www.amerevents.com/our-santas-across-usa/

Susen Mesco
Becoming Santa The Movie
4ProSantas.blogspot.com
Professional Santa Claus School
www.AmerEvents.com
303-665-8280

---

http://www.allaboutentertainment.biz/Contact%20us.htm

951-210-6464 contact phone

Located in Perris California and books entertainers and Santa for home visit, corporate parties and special events.

---

www.facebook.com/Hero4HireParty
Phone: (909) 939-0276
EmailHERO4HIREPARTY@GMAIL.COM
Website: http://www.hero4hireparty.com/

Welcome to Hero 4 Hire, we strive to be one of the premier party entertainment companies in all of Southern California. With some of the best character actors and actresses, we want to give you the best possible party experience that we have to offer.

Hire A Santa

Vancouver BC
We are proudly Canadian

We specialize in providing the best Santas you'll find anywhere. Pre-screened, experienced, reliable and naturally bearded. We are one of the largest Santa Services available in the Metro Vancouver region and we are happy to provide you with professional Santa services.

An Authentic "I Saw Santa!" Experience our goal is to provide you with the world's most authentic, real-bearded Santas.

We provide unique Santas with a wide variety of entertaining talents in Vancouver, throughout BC and across Canada and internationally.

Vancouver:
604-562-0101
Toll-Free:
1-855-562-0101
http://hircasanta.ca/

Are you ready to be an in-demand premier provider of holiday magic? Help kids dream and become a Premier Real Bearded Santa every year? We provide training and support then match you with the right client for the best possible experience.

We are looking for long-term relationships, as our customers like to have the same Santas year after year. We have a great reputation for high standards, great work ethics, high caliber suits and more required. We provide competitive wages, bonuses, WCB, insurance, staff luncheon, and proper change rooms – everything you need to be successful during the season.

We are Canada's largest Premier Santa Service providing professional, trained, reliable, real-bearded Santas. If you have any other Canadian Santas that you may have met from another province please feel free to send them our way. Come like us on Facebook, apply on line through our careers section and send us your details along with a short paragraph of why we should hire you. **Canada's largest selection of most authentic Santas.**

SantaforHire.com® is a company that provides Real Bearded Santas for Malls, Corporate events, TV and print advertisements, private parties and celebrity events. We have provided Santas for home visits, appearances at company parties and Christmas Events, to photo studios for photo shoots and Santas for TV Ads and Movies roles. We provide Santas to Department Stores, Shopping Centers and Malls from Bangor Maine, Cape Cod, New York and Miami on the East Coast and from Alaska to Seattle, San Francisco, Hollywood, Los Angeles and San Diego on the West Coast, and many locations throughout the Western USA, Mid-USA, Southern USA and Northeast USA. We provide Santas Internationally in Hong Kong and Shenzhen China and have requests to provide Santas in Macau, Singapore, Malaysia, London and Dublin Ireland.

Our Santas have been featured in many local newspapers and major nationwide newspapers including the New York Times, the Wall Street Journal. Additionally, our Santas have appeared on local and national Television Shows.

SantaforHire.com was founded in 1999 in Orange County, California and incorporated in the year 2000. We are a Talent Agency that represents actors playing the role of a Real Bearded Santa Claus and we are as an Employment Agency that provides Temporary Staffing to Individuals and Companies throughout the USA. We currently have over 200 Real Bearded Santas available for assignment worldwide. The photos of most of these Santas can be seen on our Nationwide Website: **www.SantaForHire.com** and all of our Regional Websites.

Santa for Hire.com® is Division of Internet Booking Agency.com Inc. a California Corporation. For more information, please contact us at (949) 673-7707 or e-mail info@santaforhire.com.

I'm a Santa supplier on the East Coast of Australia, New South Wales SYDNEY, Queensland etc. country & Metro Areas. I'm finding I am asked more & more for real bearded Santas.

Thanking you, Rosalind Palisi

santa@santawork.com.au
Straight Down the Line Promotions

roz@sdtlp.com.au
www.straightdownthelinepromotions.com.au
Supplier of Quality Trust & Reliability
Phone: 0411 85 0096 / 029 686 6612
Fax: 029 686 6900
PO BOX 263 Winston Hills NSW 2153

Full Spectrum Entertainment.

I Book out Santa Claus's...I am the owner of Full Spectrum Entertainment. I provide all types of entertainment all year around. I am now getting calls for Santa Claus's in S. Calif. If you still have time to add more work to your schedule, email me at:

FullSpectrumEnt@hotmail.com
Thank you, Sandee Gee

Santa in the Sand, Santa in the Wilderness and/or Santa in the Snow

Coos Bay, OR, Coos Bay, OR, Eugene, OR, Dallas, TX, Austin, TX,Kaufman, TX, Tyler, TX, Henderson, NV, Las Vegas, NV, Oceanside, CA, Temecula, CA, La Jolla Tide Pools, CA, Huntington Beach, CA, Oak Park, CA, Seal Beach, CA, Hermosa Beach, CA, and Manhattan Beach, CA. with more being actively sought and developed by the owner/operator of the new Photo group Santa in the Sand/Wilderness/Snow.

Mark DeJohn has come up with a new idea on Santa Pictures and it is one that is operating year round. Already others are trying to duplicate hiw idea but Mark is trying to tak this idea and market it in all 50 States!

mark.dejohn@santainthesand.com

www.SantaintheSand.com

Santa Schools and Educational Opportunities

There are several Santa schools across the country. Each School is different in how they approach the subject of being Santa. All of them vary in depth on subject materials and approaches to Being Santa. All of them will give you greater understanding and bring deeper depth of Character presentation to your portrayal of Santa.

The different instructors with their different backgrounds in not only performing as Santa themselves but their background as an Independent Contractor will give each school a unique flavor as they stress the points they feel is important to their way of thinking. Some will focus on the Religious roots of St Nicholas, Others will focus on how to perform in the chair they are trying to groom you for. Some schools will have multiple instructors and some will have only one.

The very fact you have this book, and hopefully the Vol. 1 book also, shows you are interested in becoming a better performer and portrayer of Santa. You are trying to learn more and become better at your craft. If you can, attend a couple of Santa schools over the course of your career. Having the benefit of multiple viewpoints will only give you a greater understanding of what it is to be Santa.

When you look at the different Santa Schools, you will see a large difference in costs and prices. A school that costs more may not be all that valuable where as a less expensive School may give you more than you bargained for. The cost of the schools is partially due to what you receive from it in the way of study materials, depth of information given during the class and the monetary value place upon the class by the owner. Do your own research into the available schools before choosing which one you attend. Read all of the materials related to each school you can. Talk to the instructor and look up some of the past students and ask them what they thought of it and why they would recommend that school over another.

You can also do a lot of research online to learn more about the character we portray when we put on the Red Suit to be Santa. This section will give you a starting place and contact information for you on several schools in the US. There are Santa Schools around the world and you have a very big job ahead of you in learning everything you should know in order to give a great performance.

The Professional Santa School of Denver, Colorado-Run by American Events and Promotions is another great school! They just had their 32nd annual school in Denver, Co. where since 1983 they have trained, outfitted and graduated over 1500 plus Professional Santas.

Susen Mesco
Becoming Santa The Movie
4ProSantas.blogspot.com
Professional Santa Claus School
www.amerevents.com
303-665-8280

—

International University of Santa Claus (IUSC)
"School 4 Santas"
"Behind the Red Suit - The Business of Santa"
Presented by Santa Tim Connaghan, RealSantas.com
Workshops are Saturday and Sunday - 8 a.m. to 5 p.m., with one hour for lunch (not included)

Basic curriculum:
Day One -
The Basics of being Santa and Mrs. Claus - plus, how to work with photo companies, malls and event producers. The History of Santa Claus - How he evolved from Stories, Legends and Cultures. 17 Centuries in 45 minutes! The Basics of being Santa or Mrs. Claus - What a Santa and Mrs. Claus should know before starting - Making the visit memorable - Positive Guest Service - your entrance or arrival - Your Ho-Ho-Ho's - Who's in charge - Who do your work for? - What your Bosses require of you.

Santa Claus Academy

Be the Best Santa You Can Be – Santa Claus Academy proudly announces that we are now in a position to bring professional Santa Claus training and education to the southeastern United States. Our experienced and professional instructors, combined with your experience and knowledge of Santa Claus will raise the level of your performance and will be an invaluable tool for the growth of the entire Santa community in your area. You will find our instructors to be entertaining and informational. We can offer one (1) or (2) day courses.

To make arrangements for the Santa Claus Academy to visit your area, please Call Gary Casey at 404-386-5554 or 770-729-8336.

Or contact me by email at **gwcasey@gmail.com**

The oldest Santa Claus school in the country. Charles W. Howard is the longest continuously running Santa School in the World. Established in 1937 and the mission of the school is to uphold the traditions and preserve the history of Santa Claus. **www.santaclausschool.com**

"He errs who thinks Santa enters through the chimney. Santa enters through the heart."

- Charles W. Howard

The CWH Santa Claus School captures the Spirit of Santa Claus and brings to life the legends and facts of Saint Nicholas. Students attending the school will be learning:
The History of Saint Nicholas and Santa Claus.
Proper dress and use of make-up
Experience for radio and television interviews
Santa Sign Language
Live reindeer habits
Practice Santa flight lessons
And much, much more!

There are many web pages and web sites that will give you a lot of information on the subject of Santa. While not a replacement for attending a school, these and many more can aid you in gaining greater understanding into the history, customs and story line of the character we play called Santa. Use the information here and in other locations to broaden your understanding and give your portrayal greater depth in your presentation. Presented for your perusal are several links and excerpts from those links to show you some of what you will learn simply by surfing the internet: Here are a few I use to start any of my wanderings when I do research in the subject.

http://www.stnicholascenter.org/pages/who-is-st-nicholas/

http://christmashistory.net/santa-claus-of-the-19th-century/

http://www.history.com/topics/santa-claus

http://wiki.answers.com/Q/Who_is_Saint_Nicholas_the_patron_...

Who is Saint Nicholas the patron saint of?

St. Nicholas of Myra is a busy saint. He is the patron of all the below:

•against imprisonment	•merchants
•against robberies	•penitent murderers
•against robbers	•newlyweds
•apothecaries	•old maids
•archers	•parish clerks
•bakers	•paupers
•barrel makers	•pawnbrokers
•boatmen	•perfumeries
•boot blacks	•perfumers
•boys	•pharmacists
•brewers	•pilgrims
•brides	•poor people
•captives	•prisoners
•children	•sailors

•coopers •dock workers •druggists •fishermen •Greek Catholic Church in America •Greek Catholic Union •grooms •judges •lawsuits lost unjustly •longshoremen •maidens •mariners •Russia •Amsterdam, Netherlands •Apulia, Italy •Avolasca, Italy •Bardolino, Italy •Bari, Italy •Barranquilla, Colombia •Beit Jala, Palestinian Territory •Cammarata, Sicily, Italy •Capistrano, Italy •Cardinale, Italy •Cas Concos, Spain •Creazzo, Italy •Cuxhaven, Netherlands •Duronia, Italy •Fossalto, Italy •Gagliato, Italy •Genazzano, Italy •Husinec, Czech Republic	•scholars •schoolchildren •shoe shiners •spinsters •students •penitent thieves •travelers •University of Paris •unmarried girls •Varangian Guard •watermen •Greece •La Thuile, Italy •Lecco, Italy •Limerick, Ireland •Liptovský Mikulás, Slovakia •Liverpool, England •Lorraine, France •Mardyck, France •Mazzano Romano, Italy •Mentana, Italy •Meran, Italy •Miklavž na Dravskem polju, Slovenia •Naples, Italy •Portsmouth, England •Sassari, Italy •Sicily, Italy •Tauberbischofsheim-Impfingen, Germany •Waal, Germany •Zepfenhan, Germany

•Is-Siggiewi, Malta	

Repentant thieves, children (especially in respect to his attribute as Santa Claus), prostitutes, sailors and fishermen, parish clerks, scholars, pawnbrokers, those falsely accused, and quite a few cities, notably Carrickfergus in Northern Ireland, with its St Nicholas Church, built in probably the twelfth century, very possibly by John De Courey. There are many other churches dedicated to St Nicholas; too many to number here. He is also the patron saint of Russia, though possibly not necessarily of non-Christian communist Russia.

Handmade and Custom Made Suits and Accessories for Santa and Where to Find Them

All right! You have decided to get into being Santa in a BIG way! No box suit for you! You wish to perform in style and comfort and strike out on your own carving out your identity as Santa in a unique fashion! Well this is the section for you!

When you decide to invest your hard earned money into a custom Suit, there are several choices to make first. What material and shade or red to use in the making of it? And for lining, what kind and color should it be? Buster Brown collar or Nehru? Standard or Coca Cola look? Workshop look or Grande Parade Suit? What style of coat? Do you want a vest? Outside pockets? Extra pants?

How about Boots? Tired of those "Round Heel Ropers"? What about a nice pair of "Bunker Boots"? How about a pair of boots built from the heels up just for you?

Now we focus on the belt. Let's get rid of those vinyl ones that came in the box with the suit and boot toppers. Time for real leather! 3-inch, 3.5-inches, or 4? Plain or with scroll work in the leather? Round buckle or Square buckle or Rectangular buckle or Oval buckle? Plain buckle or Fancy detailed?

Listed here are just a few of the many providers of wonderful Suits, Boots, Belts and other items of clothing that will set you apart from the ordinary!

http://www.wooden-nickel.net

http://www.yourtack.com/Santa.html

Leatherworx Belts

https://www.facebook.com/Leatherworx-by-Cha-Chi-128201697240918/

Custom Santa Belt

Website: **www.newcreationleathercraft.com/santa.html**

http://caprishoes.com/

http://toysforsanta.com

Eileen Strom's Private Collections & North Pole Clothiers. Please contact me at: dejstrom@att.net

www.NorthPoleClothiers.com

Personal note: I engaged Eileen in a project to make me a "magic" bag for one of my acts as a Pirate. It was a Black Velvet "change bag" with a "Compass Rose" embroidered on both sides in red thread. The finished bag was perfect in every detail. The embroidery was excellent

Santa Tim Connaghan's company

www.santaswardrobe.com

Harlequin Costume 909-390-8527

Krissi Peters owns and runs Harlequin Costume and she has made several suits for me over the last 15 years. Her attention to detail is very high and her work is excellent.

Santa Clothes--Allow me to introduce myself...By Jackie Noble
It is best to contact me by email at santaclothes@att.net.

www.sleighridermedia.com/santa_suits_accessories.htm

Santa Tom's Suits & Accessories

For serious Santas and Mrs. too!'

www.creationsbyrobbie.com/
Creations by Robbie has homemade Santa accessories

Santa suits made by Pierre's Costumes | Pierre's Costumes and Mascots
Costumes & Custom-made Santa Suits

www.costumers.com

SantaSuitOrder.com | Santa & Co. LLC –
The World's Finest Professional Santa Apparel
Sincerely Yours in the Tradition and Brotherhood of Santa Claus,
Sam Militello – owner/member, Santa & Co. LLC

Planet Santa – Custom and OTR Suits

www.planetsanta.com

sewsanta.com

SewSanta and Sewpageant
email: sherriheath53@gmail.com
Phone: 810-845-4616

http://www.sewingforsantasclauset.com/Pricing.html
We are The Sewing Elves

Little Darlin's Creations
Custom Embroidery & Tailored Sewing For Santa, Mrs. Claus and Elves

(850) 260-1880
Email: darline@littledarlinscreations.com
www.littledarlinscreations.com

Adele's of Hollywood
Custom Made Santa Suits
Santa Shirts, Vests and Accessories

5034 Hollywood Blvd
Los Angeles, Ca. 90027
323-663-2231
fax 323-663-2232
Email: adelesofh@sbcglobal.net
www.adelescostumes.com

In some cases your "custom" suit will be an Off the Rack that will be modified to your taste. In others they will be working from the Bolts and Rolls of cloth to make you a custom tailored suit. Again you get what you pay for but since these are in essence "1 of a kind" creations, be very sure your order is correct before you sign off on it.

Off The Rack Suits (OTR)

Not everyone needs or can afford a custom made suit when they are just starting out. There are all levels of quality in Off the Rack suits or as they are sometimes called "Box Suits". Just remember, you definitely get what you pay for in purchasing this type of suit.

If you are going to buy from an online source, I strongly suggest you go to a local costume "Brick Mortar" location and ask to try on one of the models there before ordering. Sizes vary greatly from one manufacturer to another. Also, you may find the suit that looks really great in the picture is not so great when you try it on.

By following this advice, you will avoid most of the problems attached to trying to return the purchase for a refund or exchange. If you buy your suit from such a place that has a real address and you can walk into to try and then purchase, you will discover other benefits from that association. By becoming a customer of such a store, they will promote your services to their other customers if you leave them some of your business cards. Online stores will not do that for you.

Try to buy the best quality you can afford and make sure it fits well. Keep the Suit in good repair and after you have gained some experience and made some money with your performance, then step up to a custom made suit and keep the one you bought as a back-up suit.

Make sure you understand the return policies. Before your order, READ everything!

Bells: **www.bellsonline.net/smallbells.aspx**

Antique-like cast Brass Bells of assorted sizes, as well as sets, including boot bells, wrist bells, hanging bells, and gift bells.

www.ToysforSanta.com

Harlequin Costume Rental

909-390-852
7780 S Milliken Ave Ste. C, Ontario, CA 91761
www.costumemagic.com/idealist.html

http://www.santasuitsusa.com/

Call Us:

(515) 274-3661, Toll-Free 1-800-383-SHOW (7469)

Write Us: Santa Suits USA, c/o Theatrical Shop

145 5th Street, West Des Moines, IA 50265, USA
Email Us info@santasuitsusa.com

http://costumesofnashua.com/

76R Derry Street, Suite 12 (Route 102) Hudson, NH 03051

Tel: 603-882-5640

Fax: 603-821-5198

E-Mail: CustomerService@costumesofnashua.com

http://www.realsantasuits.com/

http://santasuits.com/

http://www.costumesupercenter.com/

http://www.costumediscounters.com/

http://www.plus-sizecostumes.com/

www.plus-sizecostumes.com

http://www.santasuitexpress.com/

http://www.coolsantasuits.com

Claus Suit Costumes
www.coolsantasuits.com

http://www.actonecostumes.net/index.html
Theatrical Costume Shop-Adult Costumes and Children's Costumes: Costumes, Fake Beards, Costume

Encoreonstage.com
Come visit us in ...5556 Springdale Avenue Pleasanton, CA 94588 (925) 463-2140

santasupplyonline.com
Santa Supply Online (614) 726-8200
Golden Grotto
Located at 1717 Stadium Blvd, Jonesboro, Arkansas.
Telephone 870-935-8336.

These are just a few web sites and "Brick & Mortar" stores I have found searching the Internet. There is much more out there. Always remember you pretty much get what you pay for and if you buy online, be very SURE you understand their return policy. If any. excellent brands to look at would be Rubies, Halco and Fun World.

Planet Santa

Visit Planet Santa, Where the Santas Do Their Shopping

There are about 10,000 Santa Clauses in malls, stores, firehouses, and hospitals. Meet the online retailer that finds them all their duds.

BY BRIAN MOYLAN DEC 19, 2016, 9:32AM EST
Reprinted with permission by Brian Moylan

Ironically, Rich Williamson has only dressed up like Santa Claus a few times in his life. "I wore a Santa suit for a neighborhood party once and so many people were like 'our kids are asleep, could you go into the room and make a noise?'" he says. "I would bump things to make them open their eyes and say, 'Go back to sleep and get up in the morning and you'll see a surprise.' The parents were ecstatic about it."

Williamson has made a career out of bringing Santa-related joy to countless people, but it hasn't been by putting on the familiar red and white outfit himself. By running Planet Santa, the largest online retailer of Santa-related costumes and apparel, Williamson spreads suit-based cheer nationwide. This isn't a website for those who want something cute to wear to the holiday party or to terrorize sober citizens while tumbling around at SantaCon; this is for serious Santas.

The Kris Kringle costumes run from $100 to about $500, and the site's target customer is the guy sitting in the courtyard of the mall giving his flu shot a workout as thousands of tots fly across his lap asking for the latest Lego creation.

The offices for Planet Santa are in the Old City District of Philadelphia, which looks much more like an upscale shopping village than it does the North Pole. From about Halloween until Christmas each year, Planet Santa takes up the back storeroom section of Pierre's Costumes, a custom costume maker and theatrical costume rental shop also owned by Williamson. Past a trio of women putting the final touches on costumes for a regional production of Elf: The Musical and through a corridor overstuffed with every sort of military uniform, hoop skirt, and mascot head imaginable is the glorified cargo bay that belongs to Planet Santa.

It's not much, just boxes and boxes full of black boots, curly white wigs, and furry red and white ensembles to keep alive the collective delusion that a large man magically teleports down the chimney every December 24th. When I visit just before Thanksgiving, there are several stacks of FedEx boxes six feet high headed out to customers all across the country gearing up for their Christmas events. And that is just the first of the day's four scheduled pickups.

Jennifer Valosen, the general manager of Planet Santa who has been with the company for more than a decade, says that it's already sold out of the signature "Classic Look Velvet Santa Suit with Real Metal Buttons," a burgundy take on the "Coca-Cola suit," a style that was made popular by the soft drink's holiday advertising early last century. While neither she nor Williamson have actually run the numbers, they estimate they burn through about 8,000 to 10,000 Santa suits a year. That's in addition to thousands of patented boots, the best seller in the industry. Planet Santa will also unload thousands of pairs of white gloves and 500 gallons of Ben Nye Hair and Beard Whitener.

It's Planet Santa's signature suit, which it has designed and manufactured, that sets it apart.

Planet Santa offers about a dozen different suits, most of them furnished by Verona, Pennsylvania-based Santa suit wholesaler Halco. CEO Terri Greenberg says that her family and Williamson go way back and that Planet Santa is "very easy to work with." Though it's not her biggest client (she wouldn't divulge that information), the brand is one of them.

However it's Planet Santa's signature suit, which it has designed and manufactured, that sets it apart. Santa Gordon Bailey — who has been a professional "real beard" Santa for 37 years, runs the Santa and the Business of Being Santa school in Southern California, and literally wrote the book of the same name on how to be a professional Father Christmas — recommends all of his students buy one of Planet Santa's suits.

"They offer the minimum quality of Santa suit that the malls, other stores, Macy's, and just about every large photograph operation would require," he says.

That suit is made out of velvet, not the plush material that is found in older and cheaper Santa suits. It also has more (faux) fur down the front, on the collar, and around the sleeves. The benefit, however, of Planet Santa's suit is that Williamson has taken decades of feedback from Santas to give it some distinct advantages. There are four wide belt loops (rather than industry standard two) to keep Santas especially large belt hoisted around his “bowl full of jelly” belly at all times. There is also a “parade sleeve,” a bit of tight fabric around the wrists that keeps the oversized sleeve in place so it doesn’t fall down around his elbows when he waves from his sleigh. After many requests, the pants were given a fly to make them a bit easier to take off. “It turns out, even Santa has to pee,” Valosen jokes.

The pants also have pockets to keep extra candy canes (or, you know, a cell phone). But, most importantly, the suits are sized for the kinds of larger men who are typically playing this jolly and girthy fellow, which many manufacturers don’t take into account.

Planet Santa also has its own boots, which Williamson designed and has made at the same Chinese factory that makes most of the “stripper shoes” you’ll find in America.

The boots are cut especially wide not just around the calf, but also all the way down to the ankle to accommodate Santa’s larger leg and the bulky velvet pants that he’s going to tuck into said boots. “The factory kept sending us samples and we were telling them, ‘Wider, wider,’” Williamson says about designing the boots eight years ago. “They thought we were absolutely insane.” Now, of course, they’re favorites among Santas from coast to coast.

Williamson won’t disclose how much money Planet Santa brings in, but “it’s enough that it bought me my first Mercedes, and also my second, third, fourth, and fifth.” He took a bit of an odd path into the industry. He and his father bought Pierre’s Costumes in 1994 and Williamson made a website for the business in 1996, when the World Wide Web was just taking off. The site was getting tons of traffic, but they couldn’t figure out an e-commerce strategy with one brick-and-mortar shop in Philly that specializes in theatrical costume rentals and making mascots.

“At the beginning of September my father and I decided to invest $5,000 each, and if we broke even by the end of December, it was worth it,” he recalls. “We broke even in three days.”

Williamson decided a website for Santas was a good bet. Not only are Santas spending a bit more on their suits and all the attendant accouterment than the average costume buyer, Planet Santa is a seasonal business, so he thought it wouldn’t take up too much time. Williamson designed and coded the whole website himself.

“At the beginning of September, my father and I decided to invest $5,000 each, and if we broke even by the end of December, it was worth it,” he recalls. “We broke even in three days.”

The one mistake Williamson made in those early years was not buying the reverse of his URL — to this day, Santa Planet is run by a competitor. Though he no longer codes the website himself, Planet Santa still doesn’t have tons of bells and whistles, mostly because the older demographic that’s playing Santa doesn’t love the world of cyber purchasing. “I mean, we have gentlemen that send us checks through the mail still to pay for their order, because they don't do things the way we do. It’s not click, click, click, done,” Valosen says, adding that Planet Santa gets a large number of phone orders from Santas who see things online but want to talk to someone about completing the sale.

Regardless of how often the site updates, Williamson says that the business grows every year. That might be because there are fewer and fewer Santas to go around, because more and more retailers want to have the bearded one in their store. Santa Bailey says that, this year, there is something of a Santa shortage, with all of the 5,000 to 6,000 (by his estimation) “real beard” Santas getting booked so early that many malls, stores, and other outlets are bringing in lots of “traditional bearded Santas” (those that use prosthetic facial hair rather than growing their own) to give kids a warm lap.

Just like hemlines, the length of Santa hats go up and down depending on the times.

Valosen says that, along with semi-custom suits, the other trends in the industry are Santas wanting a burgundy color outfit rather than the traditional poinsettia red, and also longer and longer Santa hats each year. Just like hemlines, the length of Santa hats go up and down depending on the times.

However, she says it’s her and her staff’s willingness to take those orders by phone and walk each Santa through the changes they make that makes Planet Santa the tops in the community. “Honestly, I care about who they are, where they are, and to get them the right thing,” she says. “Even if I'm selling them the $200 suit, if it's the right suit for him, I would much rather do that than give him a $500 Santa suit that's going to be too heavy and too thick. It's the customer service aspect of it that will win out for us in the long run.”

Williamson is also happy with his place in the community, taking time to make sure every customer is satisfied and that Planet Santa has a presence at all the Santa conventions that happen throughout the year, including Discover Santa, the big convention held every year in July in Branson, Missouri. Though he only has that one memory of dressing as Santa, Williamson totally gets why these gentlemen do it year after year. “It warms your heart. It’s so corny, but it does,” he says. “If you play Santa you get such a good feeling, and I see how it’s addictive to these people. You feel awesome. Once they’re in, they’re in for life.”

Liability Insurance Sources

Once upon a time, way back in 2008, you could only get Santa Insurance from one source, FORBS Inc. Too be sure you could get entertainers insurance but at a much higher cost. That one source was one of the main reasons people joined that group. Not because they particularly like the group but because they could get the insurance relatively inexpensively.

Flash forward to 2013 and you can now get Santa insurance from a number of locations. I am going to mention several in this section. Most of the selections are various shades of vanilla but there is one major stand out and that is why I list that group first. All of the examples require you pass a background check that generally costs around $19.95 and you do have to be a member of the group you are buying insurance through. Prices stated as of 2013 or later.

1) **Nationwide Santas**

We are the ORIGINAL Santa Organization to offer

Nationwide & Worldwide Liability Insurance and Performers Insurance for non-Santa venues.

Background Check for Unlimited Single Counties - $10.00

$4 Million Liability Insurance Policy with 500k Abuse and Molest coverage with current BGC - $200.53

THIS POLICY IS VALID FOR USA AND WORLDWIDE SANTA JOBS (No extra charge for international coverage)

Add an Assistant to Santa's Policy - $83.12 (Each assistant you add is covered under the same policy at the same rate)

Additional Insurance Rider for Santas performing non-Santa venues $51.95

Year-round Insurance for other performers - $74.81

This includes Easter Bunny, Uncle Sam, Clown, Magician, Storyteller, Singer, Musician, and more

2) **IBRBS**

Level 1. $165 per year (12 months)

$2,000,000 Aggregate ($1,000,000 each Occurrence) coverage per member. Assistants can be covered for $75 additional per assistant. Includes $300,000/$100,000 Sexual/Physical Abuse or Molestation coverage.

Level 2. $200 per year (12 months)

$4,000,000 Million Aggregate ($2,000,000 each Occurrence) coverage per member. Assistants can be covered for $80 per assistant. Includes $300,000/$100,000 Sexual/Physical Abuse or Molestation coverage.

OTHER CHARACTER RIDER $75-$80! For those of you who perform as clowns, storytellers, magicians and other characters, IBRBS has arranged a new benefit; an optional rider to insure your performances. A professional first, add it on for the low price of $75 for level 1 - $80 for level 2.

Foreign Country endorsement for those Santas who will be working in a foreign country; add this optional endorsement for only $50.

3) **Clowns of Canada**

2013 cost of coverage $150 for the $2 million policy and $250 for the $5 million coverage for an additional fee you can insure your equipment through this company. HUB International

3063 Walker Rd. Windsor, Ont N8W 3R4

4) **FORBS regional**

No information was offered at time of publishing. They do have Insurance coverage to offer to their members.

5) **Society of Santa (SOS)** www.SocietyofSanta.org

SOS has no dues but they do charge a $30 "application fee" and you have a background check cost as well.

Cost of coverage $145 + $30 for a total of $175 for the $2 million liability coverage.

$300,000 molestation rider when you pass the FBI background check Insurance does cover you for other than

"Santa" performances Membership in SOS does require proof of insurance of this type. (As of 2013)

6) **LSS – Lone Star Santas**

Must be a member of LSS and have a background check. Membership in LSS requires a background check.

2013 cost of coverage $210 plus membership and background check for $4 million total amount $2 million coverage per occurrence

7) **Specialty Insurance Agency** US and Canada coverage. No Dues or fees.

SIA offers group coverage and that means the $5 million pool of coverage shrinks with each claim from any of the hundreds of Santas covered under it.

2013 cost of coverage $215 per person.

8) **World Clown Association WCA**

Must be a WCA member, dues are $40 a year

$2 million policy $139.00 a year with a $30 fee for each COI naming additional insureds (as of 2013)

9) **K&K Insurance**

No dues, Entertainer's insurance with a $5 million limit individual coverage for incomes under $30,000 a year.

2013 cost of coverage $200.

10) **AORBS Inc.**

No information was provided at the time of publishing. AORBS does offer Liability Insurance to their members.

There are many more groups and clubs that have insurance available to their membership. Just about all require the background check and with a few exceptions such as WCA, K&K, Nationwide Santas and now IBRBS you will only be covered for your Santa performance.

While having some insurance is a good thing, certain venues require a minimum level such as Bass Pro Shop, which requires a $2 million coverage policy so you have to buy the $2 million or better policy most groups offer to work such a venue

Terms and Conditions regarding Liability Insurance

There are some "terms" used in the Insurance world the following was gleaned from conversation with Steve Waters on the subject of Liability Insurance and performers. Just about every policy written for Santa Insurance no matter which group you belong to or purchase through crosses Steve Waters desk since 2008. He is an authority on the subject and will give talks to groups if asked nicely.

"Usual and Customary"

Many new performers try to cut corners by relying on their Home Owner's liability insurance. That is not a "Usual" use or purpose for that product as you are conducting business at home if performing there and you are also performing business when performing away from home.

If a claim is made against your Home Owner's policy stemming from your performance, this becomes "Known" and though the Insurance carrier may well cover the claim that one time, it can lead to raising your rate, the addition of a Business rider if available (at a much higher cost than a personal policy) up to cancellation of the policy. Using your Home Owner's insurance policy is not "Customary" for that performance use.

"Liability Limits and Assignment of Percentage of Liability"

Just because you have the insurance does not mean the insurance issuer will open up the pocket book and pay in full with each occurrence. There is an "Assessment of Liability" which they go through to assign how much you are responsible for the incident. This will be in the form of a percentage.

One example of this is where a group/chapter meeting was held in a private home. The parent group covers meetings of chapters under their Umbrella coverage as a benefit. That makes having meetings easier at restaurants and halls.

In this case there was a dog bite involving a minor child that was brought to the meeting at the home. A claim was made against the insurance for this and the insurance looked at the case and came up with this answer.

The meeting was at a private home covered by a Home Owner's policy and the Dog was living at the home in question. That split the liability involved between the Dog owner and their Home Owners Insurance and the Insurance coverage from the organization. The Dog was an "Unknown" at the time of the occurrence but the umbrella coverage made a judgment of liability and offered the amount judged to be fair for the occurrence under the rules and regulations that govern the Insurance industry. The home (and Dog) owners did not wish to involve their policy and expected the group umbrella coverage to take full responsibility for the financial costs of the child's treatment.

This is understandable but not realistic when dealing with insurance issues. The Dog is now a "Known" and is excluded from coverage if such an occurrence should happen again under the group umbrella insurance.

Group versus Individual Coverage

Group insurance coverage is attractive due to the lower cost. However the "Money Pool" which backs the coverage, but it is shared by all the policyholders.

Back in the late 80s the WCA had a group policy that all of us clowns shared.

The problem came when a few people caused claims against the coverage and drained the pool! The additional problem was the WCA did not notify the members of this! We blissfully went through the year with NO COVERAGE. Sure we had a policy and could get COIs but there was no money in the case there was a claim!

Individual coverage policies are a bit more costly but since you are the only covered performer you know if there is any claim against you and control your performance business if and when you ever run out of coverage. A $4 million package is much better coverage as an individual than a $25 or $30 million pool shared by hundreds of performers.

Finally, Performance Liability Insurance policies are a Tax Deduction. Your Home Owners policy is not.

Reasons to have liability insurance coverage.

You are sitting in a chair in the mall or at a corporate party and a child is walking holding hands with a parent but staring at you. As a result of the child being distracted by your presence, the child walks into a pillar or piece of furniture and is subsequently injured. Who gets sued? Santa.

You hand out peppermint candy canes and over the course of time the child sucks and licks the confection down to a point where the child trips or falls and the point causes injury. Who gets sued? Santa.

You give out small items given to you for that purpose by the host of the party, Candy, small toys, Bells, or anything they give you to give to the children. The child places it in their mouth and chokes on it. Who gets sued? Santa.

You have a wildly thrashing child placed in your lap and in the ensuing struggle the child manages to escape your grasp despite your best efforts to keep the child safe. In managing to free themselves they injure themselves either by their struggle or upon striking the floor. The parent is laughing as they watch this struggle and does nothing to help or ensure their child is safe.

Who gets sued? Santa.

(I now simply release the child the moment they begin to struggle. This frustrates the photographer because they have to snap the picture quickly or loose the opportunity and the parents have to chase down their child to start again.

Better to allow the child to go free than to have it injured while visiting you)

Santa is walking escorted to the break room outside the mall along the parking lot. A vehicle pulls up and stops as the driver yells “Hey! Santa!!” and allows the children to wave and call out to you. Just then the stopped vehicle is rear ended by another distracted driver. Who get sued? Santa!

In the last case, Santa is considered to be an “Attractive Nuisance” and therefore at partial fault for the accident even though he had nothing to do with the operation of either vehicle and was not performing at the time.

Most sources of liability insurance for Santa now include a rider for sexual molestation that activates once you pass the background check. This is to protect the Santa as much as the client. There is a reason you wear white gloves.

Your hands should be in view in every picture taken. White gloves help identify where and how your hands are placed at all times. If for some reason your hands are not visible in the frame of the picture, a parent could wonder, "Hmmm, where are Santa's hands? What is he doing to my child?" then you face a possible suit over this no matter what your hands were doing or why they were not in the frame.

Again these are just a few reasons to carry coverage.

For those that think their homeowner policy will cover them as they go out and conduct business as an entertainer, you might want to consult your agent and ask some rather pointy and specific questions before you find out you are not covered or have as much coverage as you might have thought.

It is also advantageous to be able to get COI is quickly and easily. Many venues demand a COI before they will allow you into or onto their property. They wish to know they have covered themselves in the event of a personal injury even peripherally involving the "*Independent Contractor Entertainer*".

There are many more groups and clubs that have insurance available to their membership than listed. Just about all require the background check and you will only be covered for your Santa performances.

While having some insurance is a good thing, certain venues require a minimum level such as Bass Pro Shop, which requires a $2 million coverage policy so you have to buy the $2 million or better policy most groups offer to work such a venue. Prices do move up or down (rarely) each year so this information on pricing may not be accurate next year. You can find more information on carriers and issuers of insurance on the "Santa and the Business of being Santa" Facebook group.

Wigs and Beards for Santa

Courtesy of Marianne F. Coleman – Handcrafted Designer Wigs

Left-Fronted yak wig Center-yak set Right-Synthetic set

Wigs and whiskers for Santa

My name is Marianne F. Coleman and I am a master wig maker. I've been a working in professional theater for 30 years. My business is called Handcrafted Designer Wigs and you can find my business page on Facebook. There are pictures and videos of most of my care tips on **www.facebook.com/handcrafteddesignerwigs** and more pictures of my professional work at

portfolios.risd.edu/gallery/Wigs/4472225

I would like to introduce you to the different types of Santa wigs and whiskers you can get.

First you really need to think about what type of Santa you want to portray. Find pictures and talk to other Santas about the type of gigs you will be doing. This is really important before getting your set. You should also factor in the cost of the set vs. the gigs that you're getting and the life of the piece. The less expensive, the shorter the life and the more expensive, the longer the life and you can also resell it in the future. You might even be able to take them off of your taxes.

The basic types of wigs are pre-made sets, custom made sets and pre-made sets with custom fronts. You can get a whole set or start with a beard and add a wig in the future. Custom sets are made to your head/face measurements on near invisible lace. The hair is hand tied individually onto the lace to look like it is growing from your head/face. It takes 40-60 hours to make a wig depending on density needed, length of hair and size of head. A beard takes 20-40 hours to make with the same factors involved. Here is a link to "ventilating"(tying each hair onto the lace). Or you can go to my page to see the video.

www.facebook.com/photo.php?v=271469229671945&set=vb.259158470903021&type=2&theater

The types of hair that you can get in a Santa set are synthetic, yak hair or human hair. Each has different price points, benefits and drawbacks.

Synthetic hair – Synthetic hair is plastic and most commonly the least expensive of the options for you. The hair is already curled, very white, can be somewhat easily maintained with a few tips and know how. They are usually long, bulky and shiny. When they are long they're up against the fur or the material of the coat and can become tangled and matted quickly. There are also different types of synthetic hair, some are heat resistant and will hold the curl in extreme heat and some will droop as soon as you put them on. The less expensive ones will give you more problems than the more expensive ones. Some can last many years with proper care. You can buy synthetics sets almost anywhere.

Yak hair – Yak hair most mimics the human facial hair texture. It's great for beards and some wigs depending on what you want to look like. A lot of the pre-made ones are very bulky, more in line with the old fashioned traditional Santa. The custom made Yak sets can be very bulky or look more natural depending on what you want to look like. The less expensive ones will give you problems like tangles, breakage and shorter life than the more expensive ones because the hair is more processed. Some can last years with proper care. You can comb and curl the hair just like you would your own. You can buy pre-made sets almost anywhere and custom made ones from me ☺.

Human hair – Human hair is just like the hair on your head but quality, white human hair is very hard to find and pretty expensive. White human hair at a lesser price is available but is so processed that it presents problems like tangling, matting and breaks easily so the life of the piece is shortened. You can comb and curl the hair just like you would your own. Depending on quality they can last for many years.

My personal choice would be a human hair wig with a yak beard to more closely mimic a real bearded Santa. I will go into more depth later on about the different types of hair and tips that you can use to keep you set looking nice.

Supplies

If you are going to invest in a quality designer wig and beard may I suggest you also invest in a few items that will prolong their life and make maintaining them easier.

Canvas wig block, in your head size, will help retain the shape of the lace, especially off-season. I cover it with clear plastic and then put clear packing tape over it so that the saw dust inside does not get wet when styling, provides a barrier to nasty/smelly stuff getting on the wig block, you can clean the lace on the wig block and makes it easier to slide the wig around to properly position it. BEFORE ordering, you should measure your head around your hairline so you can get the right size. If you have to wait to purchase a wig block at least get a Styrofoam head. MAKE SURE NOTHING IS TUCKED UP UNDER THE WIG/BEARD when you position your wig/beard every time you use it. The lace needs to lay flat or it will get wrinkled and be hard to flatten. You can also put your beard on the front. Make a mold that fits your beard out of Kleenex and put clear tape on it to attach it to the front of the wig block. Then you can work on both the wig and beard at the same time. Pictures below of how to put them on the wig block.

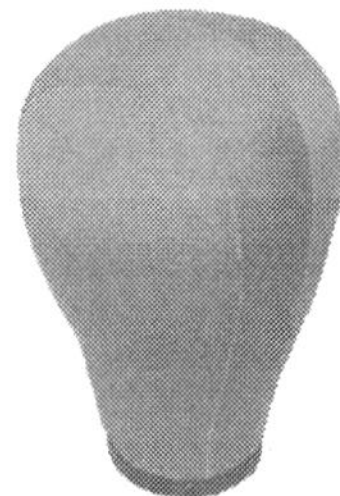

www.wardrobesupplies.com/categories/make-up-and-hair/wig-supplies/wig-blocks-and-holders

If you scroll down the page you will also see wig block holders (attach it to a table and style away) and carrying cases. My preference is Wig Block Holder Ship wheel with adjustable manikin holder for $9.99

If you use straight pins thru the lace to hold it on, make sure you put bias tape or a shoelace BETWEEN the lace and the pin. Keeps the lace from getting holes in it.

If you can't get a canvas wig block get a man Styrofoam head so the size is similar to your own head.

Other supplies:

Pik to untangle your hair

www.cachebeauty.com/Comare/markII_grippers_351.htm

Metal rat-tail comb

www.cachebeauty.com/Diane/combs/8-aluminum_rattail_comb.htm

Wool Daubers to clean the lace

www.wardrobesupplies.com/categories/shoe-care/brushes-and-applicators/applicators

Spirit gum at many vendors. I like Krylon and get it at **www.alconeco.com/**

Real chamois clothe to use spirit gum at any hardware store.

99% Alcohol and Baby detangler at any drug store.

Adhesives

I prefer spirit gum to other types of adhesives because the others are hard to work with, more expensive and rougher on the lace and hair thus shortening the life of the piece.

My concern with any of the non-spirit gum adhesives is the difficulty of working with it, the expense and the affect it will have on the lace and hair over time. Professionals who are trained to apply use them and remove the glue that can also fix or replace damaged lace and hair. They are mostly for prosthetics, which can't breathe once the glue is applied. Movies have much bigger budgets than theaters or Santas IMO.

Spirit gum – the first thing you should do with your new bottle, if it is the consistency of water, is to take the cover off and leave it off for days until it looks like honey. This leaves the nice gooey stuff behind and makes the spirit gum usable without fear of the lace popping off mid talking with a child. Yes there is a video!

When you apply SG just use small amounts (the size of a dime) in a few spots. Do not put it all along the lace; it just gives you a hard, non-flexible line that is pretty visible. I suggest dots around your temple/sideburn area for a wig and the same area for a beard along with a few spots on your chin. Practice before going to your gig so you know which spots work for you. They are always slightly different on everyone.

Put the spirit gum on your chin first – let it get tacky – position the beard, then use the tail of the metal comb to lift some hair and press until it sticks. This way the hair does not get matted to your face. Then move on to the sideburn area and repeat on a spot with no hair except use the rough side of a chamois cloth to gently tap the glue until dries. Remember to smile when doing this area so the lace does not buckle when you smile at the kids. I cut the chamois cloth into small squares.

Try out the spirit gum long before you have a gig to make sure you have the right one. Some work better than others because of different skin types, medications and heat.

I find people move on from spirit gum to quickly because they don't know how to work with it properly. When someone has problems with spirit gum I prefer to try Medical adhesive or Krylon Mastix P (good for oily and extra sweaty skin) although it can sometimes crystallize if not cleaned properly. You also have to clean the lace with acetone but CANNOT use that with synthetic hair, as it will melt off the lace. Yes you occasionally have to re-apply spirit gum but you also change shirts or suits during long hours and it spirit gum really is best to prolong the life of the piece. ALWAYS test a product on the inside of your elbow at least 24 hours before using to make sure you have no reaction to it.

How to remove spirit gum. Get a q-tip and dip it in the remover, then gently slide it under the lace and wipe it back and forth until the lace lifts by itself. You might have to use more remover to get the lace to gently lift off your skin. NEVER pull the lace off as this will make your skin raw and you will not want to put spirit gum there until it is healed. It will also damage the lace and could rip it. Yup, video on my page!

How to clean the lace on your wigs and beards. You should use 99% alcohol. Place the wig/beard on the wig block, get a wool dauber (from the supply list) and dip it in the 99% alcohol, then put a paper towel under the lace and gently rub the areas that need cleaning. If you wear makeup clean all the lace so it does not become stained. You shouldn't, please don't, have to soak the lace. That just weakens the lace and the hair.

Wig and beard maintenance

A few tips to keep your Designer sets in tiptop shape for the season.

If your synthetic set is to shiny and flash photo's look like your hair is glowing, try lightly spraying some Krylon Matte Finnish 1311 spray on it. You can get it at any craft/art supply store. A little goes a long way and you can always add more after it is completely dry. It should wash off when the set is washed and need to be reapplied. Video on my page.

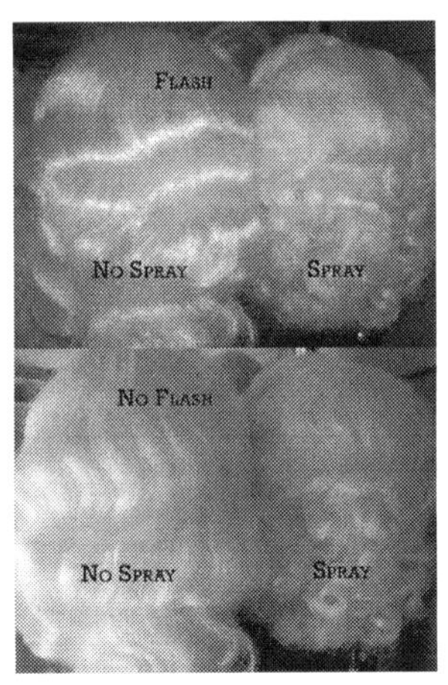

If you have your own moustache or want to color your eyebrows and don't want them to glow in the dark when a flash is used try using an off white makeup. I prefer Krylon Aquacolor #00. The color is slightly off white so you don't get the "glow" from a flash. It is water based and easy to use and remove. Spritz the makeup with water then use a toothbrush and swish it around the makeup then tap the excess off in the cover so it is fairly dry. Use the toothbrush in the opposite direction of the hair growth first. This coats the underside of the hair. Let the hair dry a few minutes and then brush the hair in the right direction. When the brush is dryish you will avoid getting blotches on your skin. Practice makes perfect! Below is a link to the company I use. Video coming soon. **http://www.alconeco.com/kryolan-aquacolor**
Even if you don't use this product get an off white to avoid the "glow" under a flash.

The proper way to attach your wig and beard to a wig block. Make a mold of Kleenex and clear tape it to the front for the beard. They can both go on 1 wig block. The beard should look like the wig with pins about an inch apart. Make sure to use some bias tape or a shoelace between the pins and the lace. This helps it retain the shape and makes it easy to work on your set. Use a pik to pik out the tangles then use a curling iron to re-curl human and yak hair. DO NOT use a curling iron on synthetic hair. There is a video showing how to remove the tangles.

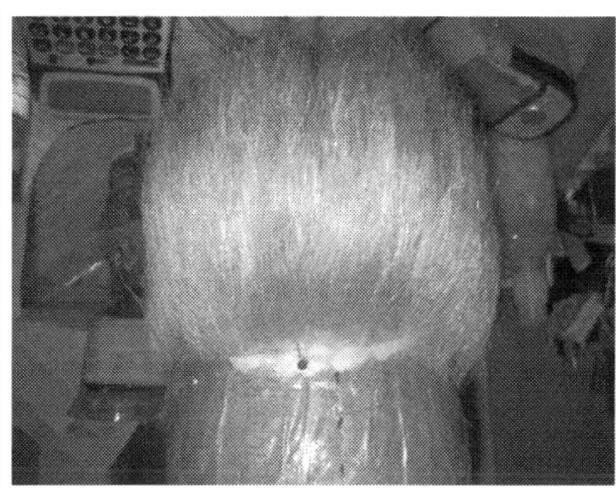

If your set gets heavy use and starts to get a little ripe you can spray some rubbing alcohol on the inside. Just lay your wig or beard down with the inside showing and spray rubbing alcohol inside. When it is dry you can lightly spray the hair. Human and yak hair curls will droop, unless permed, if they get wet, so you will need to re curl them.

You might want to get some toupee clips to sew onto the inside of the wig to help keep your wig on. You can get them at a beauty supply place. Yes there is a video to show you how to use them.

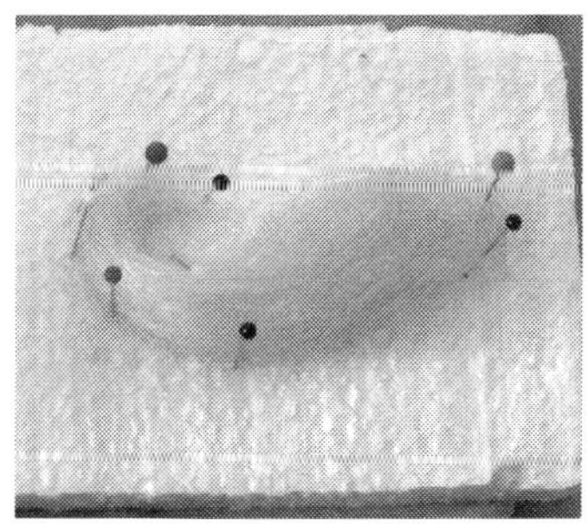

If your set is getting a bit frizzy from use you can refresh the curls. Never use a brush only use a pik or widetooth comb. Brushes make the hair frizzier and can tangle the hair. Works best on synthetic hair. Human and yak hair will need to be re-curled with a curling iron. If your set is tangled (they all get that way because of rubbing against any material) try spraying some baby detangler on it and use your pik to pik the tangles out. Start at the ends of the hair and gently run the pik down until the tangles are out then move up to the next section of hair and repeat until you reach the roots. You can get baby detangler at any drugstore. Human and yak hair will need to be re-curled. There is a video to show you how to pik out the hair and if it is synthetic you can then comb/wrap strands of hair around your finger to refresh the curls.

A tip for curling your yak or human hair mustache. Put your product on it, comb it the way you like it, fold it in half and pin it to a piece of Styrofoam or cardboard then let it dry. This way both sides are the same.

If you have any questions – just ask!

How to wash a wig/beard

Works for human, yak and synthetic

If your wig/facial hair is human or yak YOU WILL LOSE THE CURL if it is not permed. Synthetic will retain curl but be messy. There is a video showing how to refresh the curl of synthetics.

1 Remove all bobby hairpins.

2 Fill a bucket with warm water and Dawn dish detergent, a couple of squirts.

3 Rinse the wig in warm water until it is wet.

4 Put wig/facial hair in bucket and swish around a bit. Let it be for a few minutes. If it feels like it still has hairspray on it (slimy) then get some baking soda and rub it in. Let it soak for a few more minutes. Don't soak for too long because the knots of a hand tied wig/beard will become lose.

5 Rinse wig/beard under warm running water until soap is gone.

6 Use a clean, dry towel and wrap the wig in it to remove excess water.

7 DO NOT COMB. Place the wig on the wig block or styro head. Make sure no lace or hair is folded up underneath.

8 Let it air dry.

9 Once dry you can put the piece on the wig block or stryo head and pik the hair out then style as you like.

There are three basic types of hair used in wig making:

European hair: Comes in many colors and textures just like the different ethnic groups in Europe. The best/most expensive is virgin hair (see below) that goes right into bundles to be sold as is. European virgin white human hair is very, very expensive because white, not dyed hair, is very hard to get unprocessed off the head and is usually not that long nor much off of one person.

Asian/Indian hair: Which is sometimes virgin hair, only comes in limited dark colors and does not hold a curl well. This is because of the ethnic backgrounds of those people and the characteristics of their hair. If it is processed then it has been bleached and dyed to lighter colors. Therefore it is already damaged before it goes into the wig where it gets no natural oils so it is more likely to break and tangle. It might also have been put in an acid bath to remove the cuticle, which makes the hair even more damaged and fragile.

Synthetic hair: Is plastic that has been made into hair like strands. There are differences in quality that affect the ability to keep a curl and some tangle/matte more than others. There is also a heat resistant variety that will keep its curl when someone opens an oven door to remove a dish. It was developed for those with cancer and alopecia that wear wigs every day. It all depends on price and whom you get it from. The really inexpensive synthetic has a hard time retaining the curl since the strands are thinner and made from less expensive material.

Remy/Remi hair: This is a term that is used but is a marketing ploy and has no real meaning IMO. Remi hair is usually Asian or Indian and has been processed to varying degrees. Read about it at the link
http://www.royer.co.uk/remis.php

Yak hair: Comes from the tail and belly of domesticated yaks. Most domesticated yaks are dark color with some white patches. The prices vary widely depending on if it is very processed (harder to work with) to a bit processed to right off the yak. The less processed hair comes in bundles while the more processed comes in wefting and pre-made wigs/beards.

Of these hair types there are different grades of hair:

Virgin hair: Has not been dyed or permed while on the head. No acid baths or bleaching and dying, and cut by someone who knows what they are doing and keeps the root ends together. So straight off the head and mixed with other same texture/color hair.

Processed hair: Has been bleached and dyed and sometimes put in an acid bath to remove the cuticle and the root to point orientation is not kept which means you get a big tangled mess of hair after a few times of use. This hair is more likely to break, tangle and matte and there is always a question if the curl will stay for an extended period of time. Then there is hair that is dyed to match colors requested, but was not processed while on the head. So there are varying levels of damage to the hair.

Of these hair types there are different forms to purchase the hair:

Bundled hair is often virgin hair (the best, most expensive hair available); sometimes it is processed to the color needed. I have never run across bundled hair that is stripped of its cuticle.

Wefted hair is usually Asian or Indian hair that has been processed and sewn together then the short end flipped back over and sewn again to make long strips of hair more easily used for extensions and off the rack wigs. Sometimes it can be ok hair but more than likely dying or removing the cuticle, sometimes both, has processed it. I have found no way to be sure I'm getting the best wefting, especially with the cost cutting measures I've seen over the past few years. Wefted white hair has been processed since it is so expensive in its natural state.

Bundled hair vs. wefted (wefting). It's all about the cuticle and if it is present or not. If it is present the piece will act more like your own hair and be easier to maintain, last longer and not easily tangle especially when rubbing against clothing. If not present the hair will break more easily, tangle more often (sometimes to the point of not being able to comb it out) and not last as long and is a pain to deal with.

Hair needs to be all root ends on one end and natural on the other end to ensure the cuticle is all going in the same direction. The ridges all need to be facing the same way so they don't get hooked up on each other. For various reasons some hair is put in an acid bath to remove the cuticle so that it does not matter which end is lying together. When this happens hair does not act the way it should.

Bundled hair bought from a reputable company is most likely "virgin" hair. Hair that has not been processed in any way. Sometimes it is dyed or curled but you know that when you talk with the company. This is why it is the most expensive form of hair.

Wefted hair, for use in making wigs/beards, the process the hair goes through is sometimes questionable depending on where you buy the hair. It can be slightly processed to very processed by going into an acid bath to remove the cuticle. Virgin hair is never used in this form. Depends on whom you buy from, so be sure to get a reputable source.

White human hair is almost always processed to some extent since getting naturally white hair is expensive and difficult and therefore other hair is used and the color is removed which weakens the hair.

I have found the same principles apply to yak hair. Sometimes it holds a curl, doesn't get tangled or break easily but depending on form and vendor can be a mess.

I do NOT buy hair from China because it is dicey that the cuticle is still there. Lack of cuticle causes more problems and maintenance for the user and I don't wish that on anyone. There is enough maintenance involved in these pieces without dealing with unnecessary breakage and tangling.

Don't get me wrong the hair will break and tangle just not to the extent that processed hair will.

An introduction to lace: Lace is the material used to ventilate (hand tie) the hair onto

I have had some questions so here is one explanation about the different laces used.

Lace is the material used to ventilate (hand tie) the hair onto. There are different grades of lace. The names come from the history of making wigs when finer materials were not available. Generally they need to have some stretch in them to move with the performers changing movements.

Opera lace is the toughest and used in the back of wigs because it does not stretch or blend well. I tend to stay away from this lace because it is so stiff it can move the wig forward, no matter how well secured, when an actor leans their head back and the wig hits the neck.

Stage lace is a less heavy-duty lace because most theater is done to mimic real life. When there were no finer grade laces this was used on the hairline but still needed covering with heavy makeup. I use this lace in the back of wigs and sometimes the bottom of beards because it stretches and will bend with the actor's movements. The heat from the person will also make the lace conform to the head/face after a few wearings.

Fine lace was developed for the hairline area to blend in with skin tones. It is less sturdy than stage lace but does last a long time if properly cared for and depending on how the piece is built can be easily replaced to extend the life of the unseen base of the wig/beard. It is easily dyed to match skin tones, very flexible and my choice for hairlines because it looks so natural. I usually use only this lace for beards and moustaches. This is the lace that you can see in all my portfolio pieces.

Super fine lace is used for film. I have used it once but found it to be not durable enough for theatrical needs. For films you have an expert caring for the wig/beard so it would be more appealing because of how well it blends into the skin on film.

All these laces are made out of various materials: nylon, polyester and Terylene. All wig masters I know and call the material lace but veg net, caul net and power net are other names for the heavier laces that should only be used on wig foundations or very dense and heavy beards away from the hairline.

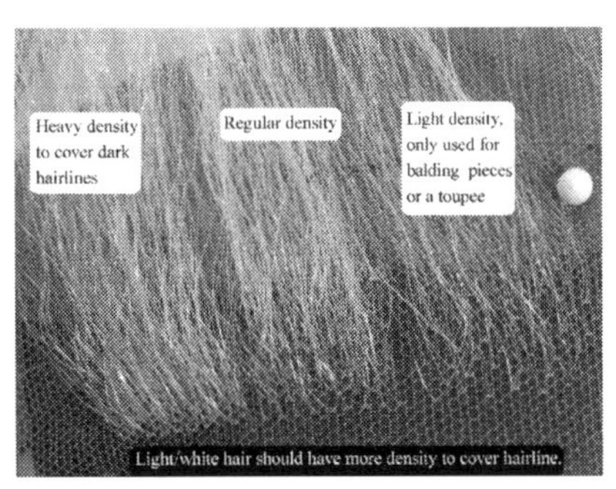

Density is the amount of hair ventilated onto the lace. This is an example of triple ventilating, regular ventilating and light density. With white/light hair you really need to go with regular to heavy density to hide the hairline.

It takes 40-60 or more hours to complete a wig depending on size of head, density and length of hair. It takes 20-30 hours to front a wig or beard because this is the area that is seen and has to have single hairs and the correct pattern to look natural so is more time consuming to do.

I've been asked why some people claim they can make them in less hours. The only thing I can think of is small heads, short hair or less density. Another possibility is the pattern/density being non-uniform, not taking the time to put the hair in different directions (yes hair has a pattern-ask your hairdresser) or tying 2 or more hairs in one hole to make up the density. Thus making it look like plugs instead of hair growing out of your head/face. COST CUTTING measures that affect the look of the piece. You know – you get what you pay for....

Hope you find this helpful and please view my work at the link and consider me when thinking of your needs for next year! Most handmade wigs and beards can last for many years, look good, and can be refurbished when sparse, and are therefore worth the investment. Marianne F Coleman

portfolios.risd.edu/gallery/Wigs/4472225

www.facebook.com/handcrafteddesignerwigs

Hair Bleaching
Featured article written by Barbara Thompkins

When I first met Santa Gordon, he came into our salon to have his hair and beard "bleached". His regular stylist had moved and I was the only available stylist that day that could do his hair. This was a learning experience for me as I had not bleached facial hair before and the thought of doing Santa's hair was very scary!

Together over the years, we have found a perfect formula for him (every Santa is different). The beard is much stronger hair usually, and the bleach can be left on longer – no heat. The hair is bleached using only the best product – no cheap stuff on Santa! The most important thing I can stress to ALL my Santas is to condition, condition, and condition!

Santa can purchase reconstructing conditioners and shampoo for bleached hair from their stylist or their local beauty supply. Also, using a "blue" shampoo helps tremendously to cut down the yellow look of the bleached hair – again each Santas hair is different, so how many times a week to use the blue shampoo depends on the Santa's hair.

If Santa does his own hair, the key thing is to follow the directions on the product and not to overlap the bleach on the new hair growth and the old bleached hair – breakage will result if it is not done properly – why I recommend a professional hair stylist with experience in doing Santa's hair and beard – you (Santa) are a professional and we stylists are professionals too!

Get good recommendations from friends for a stylist in your area that has experience in making Santa's hair snow white and then condition and treat your hair and beard with only the best products available.

I love all of my Santas and have enjoyed being the "Santa Stylist" in my salon for the last fifteen years.

Barbara Tompkins – J Randall Salon, Redlands, CA

Note: As Barbara said, she has now been doing my hair for over 17 years now, as of 2017. Before that I had a fellow named Richard King that would bleach my hair and before I was a "RBS" Richard was the fellow that cleaned and set all 25 of my Beard and Wig sets each season for me.

I have always tried to find the best people I could that would work with me to achieve the look and appearance I sought. Yes it cost a little bit more money than doing it myself but it also reaped me the benefit of their years of experience and the quality of the work they performed.

Every year I would consult with Barbara about the products and materials she would find and recommend to me for my hair care and every year I would tell others about her and the people she works with.

If you find a professional that will take you on and LISTEN to what they tell you, you stand a far better chance of getting through the season intact and looking good. Stay with one salon and preferably one hair stylist since then you will receive consistent care.

Santa Suit Construction

Featured Article Written by Krissi Peters

When thinking of your Santa suit, you need to first decide what Santa looks like to you. Most clients ask for a traditional suit when the first approach me about making them a suit. I point out to them that means different things to different people. I lived in Holland as a young child and think of St Nicholas's ornate robes, those from the Midwest think of the heavy fur suits, one client pictured the Russian Santa doll his mother always put up. All of these are correct.

You also need to consider what you will be doing in your suit, are you a mall Santa who sits for hours at a time, do you do primary home visits, are you a parade Santa riding into town on a fire truck, are you a toy maker Santa who removes his coat? All of these factors come into play when choosing your Santa suit.

Once you have chosen your look, the next factor will be the color you use to make your suit. The suits I have made over the years range from orange red to deep burgundy. All of these create a wonderful look, but how to express what color talks to you can be a bit difficult.

I have found using the embroidery thread color chart the best. It shows the colors side beside in a form that can be reproduced in fabric as opposed to paint color charts that do not always translate into fabric.

Now that you have your color chosen, it is time to consider fabrics. Looking back at what kind of Santa you are is a big help in narrowing down your choices. If you are outdoors a lot a heavier fabric with a satin lining will add to the comfort of your performance. If you work indoors, usually with no moving air, a lighter weight cotton based fabric will help keep the heat at bay.

Most of my clients prefer a velvet suit; I use an upholstery weight to keep up with the wear and tear. That being said, you can also choose silk velvet, corduroy, wool even plushy fur fabric.

For the lining of the suit I prefer to suit cotton lining, usually with a Christmas theme, this helps keep the suit more breathable. Since I do not like to put pockets in the pants of my Santa I will add extra pockets in the lining for thing little finger should find on Santa. Before I cut into the fabric, I find it best wash both the outer fabric and the lining. This helps remove any excess dyes and prevents shrinking later.

I have been asked many times how to prevent the red from bleeding into the white. I have no good answer. I have had suits laundered many times with no problem only to have red bleed for no apparent reason. Some things you can do are to only use Dry Cleaners that are familiar with cleaning Santa suit.

Most problems come from those who do not pay attention to the heat of their cleaning fluids. The heat is what caused most of the damage to the suits. It is best to check with local Santas to see whom they use.

If you are washing your suit yourself, always use a color catcher, available at Target or Wal-Mart, just in case. I have even used unbleached bar towels to catch any of the dyes that might come loose in the wash. I always wash my suits separately that way if there is a problem it only affects the one piece.

The last thing you need to choose this the type of fur. I prefer the imitation rabbit fur, in an off white color. I prefer the shorter fur to combat the problem of the fur matting. Using an off white color also helps enhance your beard, if the fur is dead white it can cause your beard to look yellow. Again this is a matter of preference, some Santas like the longer hair fur, or curly lamb fur.

In caring for your fur long term I like to use a metal-pronged dog brush. This helps keep the fur looking fresh and helps prevent the dust and dirt from grinding into the fur giving it a dingy look even when it is clean. I brush the fur against the grain to give it the fullest look. You can spot clean your fur at any time; I have even used gel bleach directly onto the fur to remove stains left by overzealous little ones.

Be careful not to get the bleach onto the rest of the suit, which is why I use gel bleach. Remember most damage to the suit is caused by heat not cleaning solutions.

If you want to give your Santa suit a bit of shine, trim or embroidery can be added to your suit. Gold button can be put down the front either on the Coca-Cola style Santa or on top of the Fur going down the front. I only use metal button, plastic just do not seem to have the longevity needed for a Santa suit.

Grand or Parade coats are a wonderful addition to any Santa. It can be made to match your suit or in a brocade or patterned fabric. Some are edged in fur and others with trims and buttons. You need to choose what suits your needs best, an overcoat, that fits over you Santa coat, or to replace your regular coat.

You can also use the longer coat to create an old world Santa look. The Grand or Parade coat ranges from knee length to floor length depending on what makes you smile. I do recommend that if you are known to be climbing up and down Fire trucks that you choice the shorter length. Nothing is worse than seeing Santa tripping on his coat. Choosing your Santa Suit is exciting; it can also be very overwhelming. Do not be afraid to ask question, get opinions and take a few chances. If you get stuck look at pictures of other Santas, you might not see the exact Santa suite you want, but you can take bits and pieces of different suit to create your own look.

Note: When having a suit made, LISTEN to the person that is making it for you. They will have specific warnings and suggestions for you as to the materials used, styles, and appearance. You can override them but you may regret your decision later. Just as in the Hair bleaching and wig making, you are engaging a professional to do a job for you and you need to tell them what you want and then listen to them if they have something to tell you. If you do, you will have a much better overall experience.

The Performing Santa

"The highest compliment any Santa can get is when someone looks at you with wide eyes, no matter what age, and says, "Oh my God! You are the **REAL Santa**!"

— *Santa True*

When we decide to bring the iconic character of Santa to life, we are creating a character that has a great many expectations upon it. Everybody has their own idea of what Santa is and is not, and how he should behave. Santa is larger than life, and by most expectations, should be excellent at everything he does. After all, he's a Saint, an Elf, possibly hundreds of years old, and magical to boot. He has almost unlimited wealth and a staff of thousands. He's magical, has the patience of a saint (original St. Nicholas not so much) and has a body of hundreds of songs, stories, books, and movies about him.

So when Santa is in front of the public or any audience, he has to both look good and sound good. For us mere mortals, bringing that character to life means bringing our A-game. This is both a blessing and a curse. People want to believe in magic and the sense of wonder and play that Christmas and Santa bring. That's the blessing. The curse is that Santa is not allowed to have a bad day. Ever.

Today's Santa is often called on to be entertaining. This is especially true if you are a Concierge Santa (a termed coined by Storytelling Santa Stephen Hollen) or a Performing Santa — one who does home visits, corporate events, and parades to name a few. These scenarios often come with a different set of expectations than the typical "Photos with Santa" and the phrase, "What do you want for Christmas?"

As a performing Santa, you will need to have different skills and a variety of material to present. From the minute you make that entrance to the moment you leave, your job is to keep Santa magical and mythical, not to let Santa turn into an old guy with a beard sitting in a chair.

So let's look at some of the things we could be asked to do as performing Santas: Grand entrances, photo scenarios/posing, personal visits such as sitting on laps, asking and answering questions, recitations and readings, storytelling, singing and leading singing, magic, acting as an emcee, dancing, puppetry, playing musical instruments, show and tell, and question and answers. All of these have performance elements in common. Some elements rely on the one-on-one interaction, others play to a large audience, and some are geared toward to the intimacy of a camera.

Imagine if instead of delivering presents, Santa was a magical plumber. On December 24 as everyone went to sleep, he would fly to your house, jump out, fix all your leaky faucets, snake your drains, and install that new hot water heater you need so badly. Santa would need to have all the right tools. He would need some serious chops to deal with all the different plumbing scenarios. And he would certainly need to know about welding, copper pipes, and roto-rooters.

Now if I said to you, "Hi. We want you to be our plumbing Santa!" would you already have the skills to deal with those plumbing concerns? Some of us might say "Sure! I'm Morty the plumber in real life!" But most of us would say, "Sorry, that's why I hire a professional."

And just like this plumber example, some Santas are already professional performers. But most of us are not professional entertainers and have not come to the role of Santa through our entertaining background.

Certainly when we put on the Red Suit, as Santas we throw ourselves into the role. But this means that we might need some new skills in our toolkits. Just being a very good-looking Santa might not be enough.

In our example, Morty the plumber can usually train alongside another professional plumber for years. They can go to plumbing conventions, learn all the latest techniques, study for certifications, and even practice plumbing in their own shops and homes.

Unfortunately, having two Santas side-by-side is confusing and contrary to the current mythos of Santa. (Interesting side note: an early proto-Claus, the Belsnickels, often ran in packs) But in our role as Santa, we usually have to reinvent the wheel for ourselves, alone. We have very little peer feedback on the job, in the line of duty. And while there might be some excellent classes or workshops to attend at some Santa schools or reunions, there are almost no weekly Santa singing, storytelling, or public-speaking classes in our neighborhoods. And we rarely get a chance to practice being Santa in front of a live (but practice) audience. When we are Santa with our clients, they expect us to be excellent because Santa is excellent. There are rarely any chances for a do-over.

Storytelling, Speaking, and Singing

Let's look at some of the foundational skills for storytelling, speaking, and singing. These are our building blocks for performing. For each of these, your voice is your primary tool. Second, your body and your physical skills come in to play. Part of being an excellent Santa includes building and increasing these skills. And finally, you need a solid repertoire of Santa performance lore from which you can build any performance with any audience.

There are three broad skill sets to hone and polish.

Visual Performance: How you appear, situational awareness, and controlling your environment.

Physical Performance: Body language, physicality, gestures, characterization, and physical interaction.

Vocal Performance: The art of being heard, voice projection, timbre, speaking versus orating, the power of suggestion.

Visual Performance

As Santa, the moment you arrive in full kit, in public, you are on stage. You are watched, photographed, and sought after. You are personally responsible for the image you project. And while you have some control over your image, you will not always have control over every scenario or circumstance. Part of building a rock-solid persona—creating and keeping the most believable Santa performance possible—includes thorough preparation and building a set of pre-performance routines.

Your performance preparation includes far more than just acquiring and maintaining great costuming. The actual performance itself requires preparation, even when you are only preparing for a fifteen-minute performance.

Exercise Assignment: Take an afternoon at home to practice assembling and getting ready to leave for a gig. Start with a complete written checklist of all the items you need to look your best for a Santa engagement. Set a timer and complete all the steps in your kit preparation. Ensure that the fur trim on your outfit has been fluffed, your clothes have been brushed, your boots and brass are polished, and your face, beard, and hair are carefully groomed. Pack any cool vest inserts, your personal snacks or drinks, and an emergency change of clothing. Assemble a full supply of candy canes. Check for jingle bells, a Santa bag for gifts, or any props used on the assignment. Complete any make-up application needed, brush your teeth and freshen your breath. See that all your bags are neatly packed; everything has been neatly packed in your car. Stop the timer.

How long did that assignment take? An hour? Longer? Did the time to complete every step from start to finish surprise you? Were there any items missing from your checklist?

It is imperative that you know how long it takes to have your cool vest inserts frozen, the time it takes to reassemble your props or candy cane supplies, and a snack bag for your own food and drinks. Your checklist is important, even when you have a rhythm and you've been doing this for years. Some days, that checklist will save you from your own exhaustion or the well meaning "help" of someone who thought they would just "move this bag for you." Your preparation time must be part of your calculation for your performance schedules.

One main reason you might not look your best is simply that you were rushed. Preparation pays for itself. Your travel time is affected by the type of traffic congestion or weather patterns (or both!) for your neighborhoods. Any modern computer-mapping program might give you accurate estimates for the current conditions, but there are always new traffic accidents or worsening weather conditions that could hit while en route. The mark of a professional includes the performer who always shows up on time (which really means shows up early), nails the performance, and most importantly, makes it look effortless and easy, every time.

Handy Santa True Tip: Use your preparation time to practice. Do vocal exercises in the shower, where the humidity and heat help relax your vocal cords and open your sinuses. Print the words to "The Night Before Christmas" and tape them to the wall or mirror. Rehearse the lines while you dry your hair and complete your final-looks in the mirror.

Now that you have a solid routine to get ready, the next key to your visual performance is the crucial moment when you arrive on-site. Before you step out of any vehicle or approach the door, build a self-inspection routine. Two tools are invaluable: Reflective surfaces and a smart phone.

Start with a visual scan. Practice a thorough review from head to foot. Pull your jacket down completely in the back, adjust your waistband, and check the alignment of your belt buckle. Ensure that your hatpin is exactly where it should be. Check your cuffs and gloves to make certain they are tugged into position. Use the mirror you stored in your Santa prep kit. Use the mirror in your car. Use the windows on your car or other cars in the area. Check your reflection in a mall window. Use the camera on your phone to snap photos or even a short video to double-check that everything is in place. Most importantly, be confident in your image. This confidence you carry helps others believe in you.

Visual imagery is important. One of the most lasting legacies you will leave is one of the strangest in modern society. You will be that anonymous Santa on the shelf in the picture of the kids. Decades later, those kids will be grown. And although no one may ever know your name (real or Santa name), one look at that picture will tell you if that Santa and photographer were on their game. This is part of your legacy, your contribution to the tradition of Santa.

Exercise Assignment: Before you go out on assignment or for any performances, get together with some trusted friends and a decent camera. Try staging your own Santa photo shoot. Recreate some of the most popular Santa photo poses. Check online before the shoot to make a list of typical images. Take some pictures with friends standing off to one side, standing behind Santa's chair, with someone on Santa's knee. Use a large stuffed animal to recreate holding a small child in your lap. Lean into a whispered conversation. Hold a small baby (doll). Pose with a friend as they try to take a selfie with their camera.

Now look at these test photos critically. How does your costume look? How is your posture? Are the buttons on your jacket aligned neatly? Is your belt buckle centered properly? Is any part of your costume bunching oddly? How does the drape of the fabric work in different poses? How do your knees and boots look in different poses? Is it time to consult with your costumer, seamstress, or tailor to fix the fit of your coat or pants? Sometimes a small repair makes all the difference between schlumpy and stylish. Check your beard in the photos: How's the color in the photos with or without a flash? Do you have any circles under your eyes? Has your beard shifted by rubbing against your fur collar? Is there glare on your glasses? Any fixes from these practice photo sessions will go into your preparation checklist.

When evaluating your practice photos or even reflecting on your professional gig images, there are always four key focuses.

Your Smile. Santa needs to smile, not just with his mouth, but with his cheeks and eyes as well. Ask your photographer to remind you, just in case. Your photographer needs to think "Smile and Hands" before every picture. And now, with everyone carrying a camera in their phones, when you see a hand come up to take a photo, be ready with your complete Santa smile.

Your Posture. Santa performances can be grueling and long. You might feel like a glorified seat cushion. Your posture will convey energy both to you and in the pictures. Adjust yourself so that nothing is binding. Move slightly forward so that you have both feet on the ground and your back is straight. Make certain that you are not shallow breathing. Make it a habit to stand up fairly regularly to keep the blood flowing and your breath going. Roll your shoulders and shake it out. Take that moment to adjust your jacket and move. These moments are good chances to wave, say hi, and get a bit of bounce back into your step. Take these moments to hydrate, as well. Hydration is very important, especially to someone wearing a very warm suit.

Your Santa Pose Repertoire. (See? Performance!) Every Santa is different, but we all have certain looks that we pull off well. Try different smiles: the surprised Santa face, the laughing super- jolly look with head thrown back (such as in Ed Taylor's photos), the regal Santa face, the mischievous playful Santa face with a raised eyebrow, looking over your glasses, wagging your finger in jest. Build a variety of favorite looks. Some will develop over time. Your goal is to be able to give a variety of expressions and poses quickly, while not looking too staged. Make a list.

Placement and Eye-line. It is very important to look at your hand placement. We want both hands obvious in the picture wherever possible. Go online and look at photos of A-list Santas and try to emulate them. Avoid having hands in weird positions, in or near your crotch, or just out of view but at unusual angles. It can be hard to tell what works best, so talk to your photographer. Likewise, when very busty ladies are in your lap, be certain that your face and head are angled so that you are looking up into the camera, not making you look awkward. This happens especially if you smile up at their face while they are on your knee. Try to lean back a bit and twist your torso away, tilting your eyes to look over your glasses. Seriously, one badly posed photo can float around the Internet for a very long time. Awareness is critical.

Remember that it is difficult to know how you look until you examine the photos. Some of your smiles might make you appear to squint, especially depending on the height of the chair or the camera height. Some photos may look better if your head was tilted the other way. You might want to experiment with thc twist of your torso.

Every time you work with a photographer, try some test shots at the beginning. Take a look and get some feedback. After a group of photos, ask your photographer to look at them critically, and ask if you can see them yourself. As needed, reset your posture and poses before the next batch. If you perform a home visit, always ask if they can send copies of photos to you. This helps you keep track of how you are doing. And, with their permission, you can collect some nice photos to help you with your Santa marketing.

Knowing how to take good Santa photos and how to orchestrate good photo placement is very important, especially in scenarios where you are visiting a hospital or a private home. The experienced Santa knows when to step in with some careful suggestions. Most people have cameras with them and they do not always know where to stand to take good photos or how to set the shot so that Santa and friends look well framed. This is where the photo-experienced Santa comes in. Let's look at an example.

"Ho-ho-ho! Momma Jackson, why don't we take one of those sturdy, straight-back dining room chairs right there and put that green plaid throw over it? Shall we move Santa away from the fire and sit over by the Christmas tree, away from all that reflective glass? This way you won't have flashes bouncing back in the photos. Tim and Tina, could we move some these presents over here? Maybe we can have the teens stand on either side of me, and we could put Fluffy here on the footstool right next to me? Could we could put little Nellie in my lap for the photos? Mrs. Jackson, what if you stand right there? And after you get some good wide shots, would you like to step in to get some close-ups, too? How does that sound? Shall we turn on this lamp? Ho! Excellent! Now everyone will see what a beautiful tree you have!"

Months later when that client comes back to you and says, "We took the most amazing photos of you!" then you can nod and smile and say, "Amazing! You have a great eye! I hope you shared them!"

You will also note that in this example, Santa did the following:

Phrased everything as a question.

Got away from the roaring fireplace, to avoid being a sweaty mess.

Arranged proper seating, so as to not to be in the Santa-eating chair.

Distanced everyone from inadvertent reflections.

Made it all look pretty.

Arranged it so the teens could stand alongside him, and the dog was not on his suit.

Involved everyone.

Turned on an extra lamp, so there was more ambient lighting so the auto-focus would work.

Santa Sneaky, eh? This is a subtle part of controlling the Visual image you want to project, but an important one. Photographs are part of your visual performance. And while we are discussing performing photographs....

Video cameras are now part of most smart phones and most digitals cameras, whether point-and-shoot or DSLR cameras. If you have a situation in which many people are videotaping you at the same time, make certain your energy is up. And if you like, nod toward the camera, as if acknowledging it. But your primary focus remains being genuine to the people you are in direction interaction with. Occasionally, you will run into people who want to direct you or videotape every last bit. It adds a different dynamic to the situation. This video could be up on YouTube very quickly. So always be polite and carefully stay in character. If you focus on creating a relationship with the people around you, it will look genuine on camera. And it is okay to say something like, "Did you get enough video? I want to make sure you get a chance to relax, too! Why don't we turn off the cameras for a bit while I get situated, and I will remind you when to turn the cameras back on? Wonderful!"

Speaking of cameras, video technology has grown. Now people can easily pull up Skype or video messaging software and ask you to record a message or talk to someone via a video link. Be careful. This is where Santa's all-knowing omniscience can fail you. Suddenly you are talking to a little girl who wants to discuss "Mipsy" (their elf on the shelf) and you have no clue. What about her dog? Her sister? And so on. So if you agree to speak by video, set some conditions engage the other person as your co-conspirator. Find out the following and set the rules.

"I would be delighted! But I can only do this for a short time, I'm afraid. Let me say hi to these folks over here, while you get the video ready. And what can you tell me about the following? Tell me about your relationship, who we will we be talking to, how old are they, have they been good? Is there anything they could improve on, did they do anything really well this year? Is there an Elf on the Shelf in their family, and if so what is its name? Have they sent Santa an e-mail or letter this year? And is there anything else special I should know?"

Note that the Santa is not sitting there while the person is trying to lock on their Wi-Fi, get the app going, or clean their lenses. Suddenly they realize that you, as a Santa performer, are giving them something of value. Then the video recording can be shaped something like this.

X is right here and they wanted me to say hi! I am delighted to see you.

Are you excited about Christmas? Santa is so excited about Christmas; it's my favorite time of year!

________ have you been a good boy or girl? You have? Wonderful, keep up the good work!

Well, I will be delivering a special present for you soon on Christmas. And don't forget my cookies and milk, and don't forget, my reindeer love carrots!

X, thank you for letting me talk to them. And, MERRY CHRISTMAS!

If the people on the other side of the phone want to keep it going, you can tell them that Santa has to take care of things where you are. They can send you an Email or a letter, with their parents help, of course.

Your goal is to delight the person taking the video, and the amaze the recipients. Make certain you hand them a card at the end of it.

Visual performance is also part of live performance, not just for the cameras. One of the most important things you can do as a pro-Santa is gain situational awareness and the ability to control your cnvironmcnt. Hcrc arc somc kcy things to remember and some examples.

You are the Pro Santa. You are responsible for how you want to be seen. And while the client may have some experience, you are usually the most experienced Santa in the room. "Hello Mary, I just happened to notice your pets are getting really excited. Could we have them put in another room for right now? I don't want to scare them."

Establish your expertise. By taking charge, you are helping the client get the best experience out of what they are paying for. "Hi Mike, this looks amazingly wonderful! You look like the person in charge, and as this is not Santa's first sleigh-ride, I just wanted to ask you a question or two. I see tables full of sweets and video games but not very many adults. We will need adults to supervise the kids. Santa is not a baby-sitter and I cannot take photos with them in my lap without the parents being in the room with us. Any thoughts?" In the above statement Santa has done three things. He's established his concerns, made the person he's talking to feel in charge, and done it in the form of a question so it is not threatening. By stepping up and asking questions, Santa has just prevented a screaming three-ring circus, because the parents indeed had planned on going into another room for drinks. It happens.

You cannot control everything. Sometimes you just have to roll with it. But here's a tip you can use from improvisation classes in theater. They use a rule called "Go for the agreement." This means that if someone hands you an imaginary frog, your character does not say, "No, it isn't. It's an apple." That kills the scene and the momentum. In Improv, you say, "Yes! And..." In this case the performer keeps it rolling by saying, "Yes, a frog! Mortimer, you singing dancing frog you, how have you been?"

Santa is playful and fun. And people want a chance to have fun. Even adults! Let's say for some reason, they have parked you and your Santa chair right next to the door to the restaurant kitchen. There's no way for you to get them to move you in the time allotted. Staff flies in and out, and it's really awkward. Ignoring it will be hard. So a creative Santa can ask all the kids and folks to be his co-conspirators. You could say, "Every time one of them comes through, I want you to turn your head and say Merry Christmas! And then turn back to me, right away!" A few fun "Merry Christmases" later, the disruption has been acknowledged and becomes second hand. Pretty soon all the wait-staff are in on it, and everyone in the place is hearing a regular, "Merry Christmas" from the corner.

Santa is strongest when he is genuine and fun. So make the best of strange situations. Here are some places where your Visual performance is going to get noticed.

Grand Entrances. When Santa comes into a room, he comes into a room. Ask your escort what is ahead of you. You might hand them your bags and arrange your jacket and parade coat. Or you could hand them your jingle bells while you enter slowly—large and in charge. After you've made eye contact with everyone and thanked them for inviting you, then go around and shake hands with everyone while you re-introduce yourself.

"Hello! (shake-shake) My name is Santa, pleased to meet you!"

Why do both? Two good reasons. First, when you first come in, your visual image is striking. You worked hard on your image and you want folks to get an eyeful. Secondly, the up-close and personal is establishing the social contract in which we agree that I am Santa Claus. The psychology of that moment is wonderful, if a bit hidden, because deep down, a tiny part of them in the back of their head is asking, "OMG, what if this is the real Santa? I am shaking hands with SANTA!" This adds excitement to the moment.

Smaller Entrances. If you are dealing with little ones in a family setting, you may want to dial it back. Shake hands with the adults. And if you have one kid who rushes to you, go down to a knee (if you can) and pull them in for a hug.

Afterwards, ask them to take you by the hand and lead you into the room. "Can you show me your Christmas Tree?" Also, bring down the volume. And when you are talking to the client before you show up, make certain that any excitable animals are going to be kept locked up for the duration.

Parades and Public Events. If you are moving, be very aware of where your coat, hat, and any accessories are going to be. If you are riding on something, place yourself where you can brace yourself and where people can get an unobstructed view of you. Be prepared for sudden stops or wind. Gestures should be all upper body and large. If possible, get a sound system with a headset microphone and light colored windscreen. Make certain the speakers are not immediately behind you, to avoid feedback. Try to find out what the local populations are (for instance, Spanish or Danish) and learn how to say Merry Christmas in those languages.

Public Areas or On Streets. First, never let Santa be a traffic hazard. Be especially carefully around kids or folks who might rush to you. You never want to accidentally endanger someone, so situational awareness is critical. If possible, in public, always have an assigned handler (it could be an Elf, a friend, a security person). Survey your area. If you are performing in the round (audience on all sides), make certain that people are not going to accidentally flip over benches, chains, or fences. If the ground is muddy or slippery, you might be fine (since Santa is wearing boots) but others might not be. So, please be aware for your audience.

Good Lighting. Your goal is to get a medium level of overall lighting, with a bit of back light and some good front lighting. Too bright can make your face and beard look washed out. Too dark, and many cameras won't be able to autofocus, and your costume will look dark and muddy (especially if it's a plush burgundy). Pay attention to audio as well. Avoid areas with a heavy background noise, or super hard reflective surfaces (which are problematic for both light and audio bounce back). Areas with natural greenery, warm tones, wood, or rocks look good in photos.

Handy Santa True Tip: If you are ever need a quick generic background for photos or headshots, find a wall full of healthy ivy. It's a natural backdrop. Likewise, a stand of pine trees with nothing else obvious in the background can be very Christmas-y!

If you are working in a mall or shopping center, be aware that in a busy place, you will get stopped for "just one photo." This can then turn into a hundred, and you will make a snail's pace to where you are going. (Ask any Mall Santa about this.) That's why Mall Santas are often escorted by elves or security.

But often times, you've just shown up to a gig, solo, and you are trying to get to where you need to be. This is the time to break out the industrial strength Jolly and just keep moving while saying, "Merry Christmas! Why thank you! Yes, let's take pictures, I'm headed to my chair!" Don't do this loudly, just conversationally.

Other visual moments. Santa is iconic. So if Santa participates in photo bombs when people are not expecting it, this can be a ton of fun and a great way to be noticed, especially when you don't seem to have many folks visiting you in the chair. Just be prepared to do more traditional photos after you do. Likewise, if you run into authority figures, have an extra Santa hat handy or pose for a "back to back" photo. For smaller visual moments, when someone spies you getting in or out of your car, just give them a wink and the finger on the lips—it's a secret!

If you want more ideas, go online and search "Santa Claus News" or "Real Santa Claus Photos," then look through the images. As you page through the search results, look closely at the pictures of Santas with problems: Wrinkled costumes, bad posture, odd lighting, or strange beards. Now look through the photos again for the successful Santa images: Great eyes, good posture, and other things stand out. Look for "dynamic" images that look alive and "genuine" contact between Santa and the camera or Santa and other people. Your goal is to always appear solid and excellent. You will want to use your visual templates—your poses, ability to work with your environment, your facial expressions—with ease and consistency.

Physical Performance

Your physical performance includes body language, physicality, gestures and characterization, and your complete physical interaction.

As mentioned earlier, Santa is an iconic character. Everyone has an idea of how Santa should look, act, and behave. And over the years, especially through advertising, we have seen Santa do everything from skateboarding to cartwheels. But most people dismiss that as "Hollywood."

But let's take a moment to think about the lore. Santa is magical. His delivery night is beyond human capability. He must be powerful, if only because he drives a sleigh and carries a big bag over his shoulder. He's tough enough to live at the North Pole, devour metric tons of milk and cookies, and run the biggest toy company in the world. So our character can range from an older obese man in his 60's to a magical being capable of almost anything. But the truth is, we are mere mortals who portray him, and we often do not have amazing capabilities. Furthermore, when Santa seems to have typical human frailties like a bad back, bum knee, gas, or a cold, it tends to humanize him and takes some of the magic away from our portrayal. But there are ways we can use our physicality to portray him in ways to help build belief and magic.

Exercise Assignment: One key method for getting into the skin of a character is always give your character something specific to do. Let's take a character from a fairy tale, the Big Bad Wolf. Take a few moments and try some exercises around the house. How does the Big Bad Wolf brush his teeth? How does he eat a sandwich? How does he worry about something? How does he react to a big bill in the mail? Try several tasks, use your imagination, and have fun.

Notice anything about how you expressed yourself? Was your big, bad wolf low and growly? Was he more of a slick-zoot suit kind of guy? Or was he harried and a hen-pecked sort of bad guy? Were his actions tight and focused, or relaxed and loose? Was he continually ready to pounce or just kind of annoyed?

In theater and in storytelling, characters often use a key gesture or phrase. By playing with our characters, we discover mannerisms, vocal expressions, and physical traits. This can be a tool for you, too! Admittedly, if you are Santa for ten hours a day in a mall, the lines between your expressions and those of the Santa are going to get pretty blurry. But say you were doing a home visit, a corporate event, or an audition.

Being able to call up that key gesture or phrase will help you lock into your character and help you bring him to life. Even if you yourself are not having a good day, or you find yourself a bit tired or nervous, knowing how to get "in the skin" of your character can be really helpful. Your key gesture could be as simple as hooking your thumbs in your belt, leaning back, and chuckling. Or perhaps you sing the opening of Rudolph the Red Nose Reindeer.

Here are some other tips on physical performance.

Think from your audience's point of view. The size and scope of your physical gestures will vary depending on where you are and what you are doing. If you are in a Parade, you want your gestures to be broad and smooth. If you are at a home visit, move your gestures from the center of your torso out, and be gentle if you have many small children about. If you get a chance to experiment, sit down with someone else playing the role of Santa and look up. What do you see? How will children see you? If you are in a public venue, will only the front ranks be able to see you? Is there anything you can do about that?

Body Language. When you search for images of Santa on the Internet, it's easy to see both good and bad body language. One of the key problems is slumping. Often the chairs provided for Santa are too deep. Very imperceptibly, when we wear a hat, beard, and/or glasses, our heads tend to come down and our shoulders to roll forward. Teach yourself to monitor your posture on a regular basis.

When seated, Santa should be in an "open" position: feet and legs apart, leaning slightly forward, head tilted, and hands relaxed.

Learn to read your audience: Are their arms crossed? Do you see hand clenching or wringing, or possibly foot tapping? Learning to read your audience can help you target the right performance at the right time. Keep in mind that different cultures have different styles. In some cultures, touching is very common whereas in others, touching is reserved for specific relationships.

Micro-expressions. Did you know that we all have tiny expressions as well as body language that convey our feelings? If you are exasperated and your smile is forced, you will have a tiny expression flit across your face. People are quick to pick up on that, even if it's subliminal. Many Santas are pretty good at picking up on that, too.

Take some time to do some people watching. Notice how people show confidence and playfulness, and attentiveness. While standing, a confident person has feet firmly planted, shoulder width apart, shoulders are back, head is still, and arms are held lightly to the front. No fidgeting and movements are steady. Also, talk a bit slower and take good-sized strides, survey your domain. Now, look at playfulness, engagement, and attentiveness. What do you see?

Learn to make sincere eye contact. Also learn where eye contact can come off as aggressive.

Body Language. Santa is one of the few roles in today's culture where touching still happens. Folks sit in laps and give hugs. Take advantage of this (but not in a creepy way). Shake hands and introduce yourself. This creates a "buy-in" and closes the physical space. Santa can pat someone on the back during a laugh; take both of someone's hands in theirs as a gesture of sincerity. Children often times want hugs.

Learn how to do this with one leg forward when they come flying in, and offer a warm one-handed hug or pat.

There is so much to learn about physical performance and about reading other people's body language and micro-expressions, you would be amazed. Watch the best actors: they can create a character with a prop, several words, and just a few actions. It's amazing. But remember, from the moment you were born, you've been studying other people. You are much better than you know at picking out subtle things. You can you use this to your Santa advantage.

Vocal Performance

Your vocal performance includes volume, projection, tone, pitch, enunciation, and diction, among other details.

What does Santa sound like? What does Santa sound like? Ask yourself. Go ahead, we'll wait. You might say something like, "Jolly, baritone, bass, rumbly."

Human beings learn in a variety of ways, whether that's visually, aurally, kinetically, or a combination of these methods. Chances are, at some point in your life, you keyed in on a Santa that just made the moment for you. And forever more, Santa, the real Santa, sounds like that memory to you. Often times, we use movie memories that come to us from Hollywood. Some of the most famous Hollywood Santas had very distinctive voices. Those voices came to them by the way of years of acting or performance training. When we hear the gruff growl of Ed Asner, the snarky tones of Tim Allen, the various complex tones of Tom Hanks, or the cultured voices of Richard Attenborough or Edmund Gwenn, we are listening to some of the best of the best. And you may need to forgive folks if they want you to be just as good as a trained actor who also had a host of audio technicians, mixers, and sound men plus some great writers behind them.

Here's the good news: As Santa, we create our own little reality. Make a good first impression, get buy-in from your audience and, voila, that other memory gets pushed to the back.

Santa is at first a visual figure. He's very striking and brightly colored. But then, as soon as he comes in and makes a grand figure, we find ourselves anticipating the hearty "ho-ho-ho!" At the end of the evening, Santa wraps up with a great big, "Meeerrrry Christmas and to all a good night!" It would be very odd if he sounded like Daffy Duck. A great vocal performance is the jelly to our peanut butter, the cheese to the cracker. Things like this help us nail our recreation of Santa. And vocal ability takes consistent, ongoing PRACTICE.

First, let's be clear: Everyone has a natural voice range. This range can be expanded with training. Training also improves volume, projection, timbre, and singing on key. Your voice is created by a set of muscles and attributes. Very few people are born with a voice like Patrick Stewart (Jean-Luc Picard), who could read the side of a cereal box and people would pay him good money to do so. He is also a classically trained Shakespearean actor, emphasis on the word "trained."

Our goal as Santa is to give our natural abilities a little extra oomph. Even if you have a high-pitched voice, or perhaps it seems raspy, or you have an accent—your natural voice is fine. If you continue to work on speaking and vocal technique, it will pay off big time down the road.

Here are some specific things you can work on to improve your vocal performance.

Be Prepared and Practice. Why? Because uncertainty brings stress and your audience can pick up on it. Stress reduces your vocal capability. Confidence in your material helps you relax. And people pick up on confidence, too!

Breathing. There are any number of breathing exercises that can help you develop greater volume, projection, and airflow. Increased airflow helps your stamina. If you are trapped completing a 20-minute performance in a noisy room for a large audience, vocal stamina really pays off. Breath is life. Your goal is to let your breath always come free and easy, with no tightness.

Flexibility. You want to stay loose during your performances. Before you perform, always loosen up for a bit beforehand. Use a quick set of both physical and vocal exercises to warm up—it will really help in the long run.

Position and Posture. How you are standing or sitting can make a world of difference. One of the nice things about being Santa is that we can let our bellies out, taking advantage of our natural diaphragm. Practice your best standing and sitting vocal positions.

Pacing. When we are nervous, full of energy, or stressed, we tend to speed up. This then affects your natural tone, musical key, and how fast you complete your performance. When you practice, record your rehearsals. Try a variety of speeds. If you typically perform, "The Night Before Christmas," try it fast, medium, and slow. Time yourself. Later in performance, if you know that you only have a specific time limit, you'll already know which speed to use for your recitation, story, or song.

Sincerity. If you sound too forced, staged, or pompous, you will lose your audience. Part of the key is making great eye contact and speaking to a person, genuinely. Warm tones work best in closer environments like home visits. Know what you want to say and care about it.

Pitch. There are a variety of websites and tools you can use to make certain are you are singing in key. Santa can carry a pitch pipe or have a pitch pipe app on his smart phone, very easily. When we sing, we can be either sharp or flat on a specific note. Sometimes our own ears betray us: We might think we are on pitch when we are not. Seek out friends or family that have musical training or look for a vocal coach or choir director who can help you evaluate your skills.

Inflection, Emphasis, and Rhythm. Take for instance the verse for "5 Golden Rings" in the "Twelve Days of Christmas." Everyone belts out, "Fiiiiiiiiiiivvvveee Gooooooolden Riiinnnnggss." If we did that same emphasis for, "Threeeeeee Frrrreeeeennnchhh Heeeeennnns," it would sound rather odd. Whether we are singing, storytelling, or doing a reading, we have a variety of speeds, rhythms, and emphasis points we can use. See the exercise, "Twas the Night before Christmas."

Volume and Projection. Volume is a physical measurement of how loud we are. Loudness is also a relative term. If you are yelling in a loud factory, it may not even be noticed. Knowing how to gauge your volume in various environments is a learned skill. Voice projection is the strength and quality of the voice, paired with an ability to be heard clearly. A person who has trained at projecting their voice uses less energy and can be heard more clearly. The quality of their voice is more resonant and robust. Voice projection requires clear breathing and a good stance, as well as an understanding on how our vocal apparatus works. You may need to seek out a trained vocal professional for assistance with projection.

Articulate. Just like warming up before doing physical work, you can warm up with your vocals before you perform. Try some tongue twisters, singing scales, or rehearsing some pieces that are challenging. Articulation is especially important if your voice is naturally in a low register. If you have a strong accent, specific speech issues such as stutter, or if you have dental issues, doing a few vocal articulation exercises as a warm up is an excellent idea. Try recording yourself. Have someone help you listen critically, to see if you have any verbal issues that you might want to address.

Exercise Assignment: There are many verbal or articulation exercises available on the Internet. Try this tongue-twister for the letter B. "Betty bought a bit of butter, but she found the butter bitter, so Betty bought a bit of better butter to make the bitter butter better."

How did the tongue twister work? What other practice phrases make you focus on the consonants and vowels in your speech?

Exercise Assignment: Try reading "Twas The Night Before Christmas" through, as basically as possible. Now do it again faster. Then do it again, but this time shake it up a bit. Emphasize some lines but not others. Do some as whispers and some really loud. Then do it again in character, not just Santa, but as a little kid, or a sleepy adult, or with an accent. Have fun with it. Now, take all those experiments, and hold the book to your side and present the story while pointing to the pictures. Try to maintain as much eye contact with your (imaginary) audience as possible.

Which reading had the most meaning to you? What did you discover that seemed like a new, great idea? Which reading gave you the most trouble? Which seemed the easiest?

Handy Santa True Tip: You can videotape yourself and then give yourself feedback. Also, take some copies of songs that you want to sing with you, and play them in the car just before the gig.

Storytelling Basics

First, consider that we are all storytellers. All of us learn through stories, tell stories, and enjoy stories. It is one of the first art forms and has had a profound effect on humanity. Some of humanities greatest influencers were storytellers: Abraham Lincoln, Mark Twain, Jesus Christ, Buddha, the list goes on and on. Anyone can tell a story. Learning to be a master storyteller can take a lifetime. We can't cover everything, but we can explore some questions and suggestions about the art that encompasses myth, folklore, legend, fairy-tales, and tall tales,

Stories and Santa. If there is one character in modern Western media that is a better example of the power of storytelling than Santa, I am hard put a name to it. Christmas (outside of religious connotations) is a huge cultural movement and industry in Western society. Anyone who knows about the history of Santa Claus and his various elements—from St. Nicholas of Myra of Turkey to the Yule influences, to cultural influences from the Norse, Celtic, and Anglo-Saxons—know that Santa is an amalgamation of folklore, myth, religion, marketing, and creative advertising.

Not only is the story of Santa one that we still share and celebrate every year, it is ongoing, changing, and evolving. And every professional Santa is bringing those stories to life, which is pretty amazing. If we look at the societal role of Santa, his role in a very traditional sense could be called shamanic or priestly. He is magical and identified by his clothing, hairstyle, and annual ride. We trust little children to him, he has a judging role, and he lives outside the bounds of normal society.

In nearly all early cultures, people who understood the power of story filled that quasi-religious role. That story could entertain but also create truth, understanding, and cross cultural boundaries. So it should be no surprise that our modern Santas should be one of the few roles where it's okay for Santa to come in and share some stories.

At this point, let me make a distinction. There are all sorts of stories, storytellers, and storytelling techniques and story props. But for our purposes, let's define storytelling as a story that we would tell without the use of book or reading something. If you are reading a story from a book, you are doing a recitation or a reading. (This can be entertaining, but is not storytelling per se.)

So what do we mean by storytelling?

Storytelling happens when we share a story that has a beginning, middle, and end. It is told directly to the audience and direct eye contact is made. While Santa can be telling a story about his life and events, he is not an actor but he is relating something.

Why tell stories? For lots of good reasons.

Santa lives because of stories.

If you are a great storyteller, you can captivate audiences and share a skill that we don't get enough of these days.

You can create your own stories, unique to you, tailored for your audiences.

Stories pack pretty easily.

A good storyteller does not need a lot expensive props, instruments, etc. You can sit down, and ask, "Do you want to hear a story from Santa?"

Storytelling is good for kids. Science has shown that the ability to follow oral narrative and actively visualize it is great for cognition among a host of other skills. To paraphrase Albert Einstein, "If you want your children to be to be intelligent, tell them fairy tales. If you want them to be more intelligent, tell them more fairytales."

The messages you share in your stories can not only strengthen people's belief in the values of Christmas Spirit, but a story is a shared journey that everyone, young or old, can go on.

Learn to be a good storyteller and you might find you have saleable skills throughout the year! One of the great things about being a storyteller, there is no mandatory retirement age. And having a long white beard is not such a bad thing! Storytelling is an amazing tool for communicating effectively, and it can be used in a variety of ways. Storytelling is important to public speaking, sales, grief counseling, working with at risk kids—you name it. [For more on storytelling, check out the National Storytelling Networks, A Beginners Guide to Storytelling (a handy little book).]

First, how do we choose a story?

Listen. Believe it or not, spoken word is still being done. You can go to storytelling events, watch storytellers online on YouTube, and attend storytelling events. It is considered bad form to completely copy another teller's stories without permission. But most traditional stories have multiple variants. Look for other versions and create something that resonates with you. You can also perform personal stories from your life and stories you created.

Read. Hundreds of traditional stories and created stories out there. Be careful when looking at something that has a Newbury or Caldecott award, or something from Disney. Make certain when you perform that you make it your own. If you perform something that is part of a trademark, you could have issues. If you are looking for traditional stories, August House lists many good resources at **http://www.augusthouse.com.** Try searching the Internet for "traditional folk tales." You will find a variety on the web.

Evaluate. Every story has pluses and minuses. It has a "Most important thing" (often times a message), plus the characters and plot. Every audience and event is different. Picking the right story, for the right time and place, takes practice. Generally, the younger the audience, you want to make it more interactive (like call and response), less scary, and maybe more funny. Older audiences enjoy more dramatic, insightful, clever stories. But the great thing is that as your repertoire grows, your ability to reach out to your audiences will, too.

Grow. As you tell your stories, you will discover things that audiences laugh at or the places where you seem to lose them. Some sound effects and gestures work or don't. Your story will talk to you and change as you tell it. Plus your skills as a storyteller will shift as you develop your voice and style. How can you grow as a storyteller? Always look for new stories, new opportunities to see other tellers, and new chances to tell to new audiences.

Get to know your story. Most stories have something in common: Plot, struggle, goal, resolution. Learn the story sequences. Look into what's called "the Aristotelian Theme." There are a variety of ways to map out your outline. Try working on a storyboard or a traditional outline. Spend time with each of your characters. Some characters are very one-dimensional. Others have very specific voices or mannerisms. It really helps to know their key gesture or phrase. Doug Lipman, storytelling coach extraordinaire, speaks about the concept of "MIT, or Most Important Thing." The MIT is usually the thing that drew your interest in the story in the first place, the thing that for you drives the story. Knowing your MIT really helps. Many stories also emphasize a message. Rudolph the Red Nosed Reindeer has strong message—or several. What do you think that message is?

Know your audience. This is just as important to a Santa as well as a Storyteller. When we do performances, three things can really help you.

Do your homework. Find out everything you can about your clients and audience. Your best source of information is the person who hired you. Interview them to learn as much as possible: your audience members' ages, what have the people have been up to, what they are expecting, other things that they have done—the whole "who-what-where-when-why-how" comes in handy. Let them know that the better they inform you, the better you can tailor your performance.

Research. You can do some research on-line and by networking with others who have worked with them.

Arrive early and investigate. On-site, it's always a good idea to get there early and chat folks up. Of course, as Santa, you have to stay in character, but making friends and asking questions can be really helpful. In some cases, you can always do a little early research off the clock as a non-Santa person.

Using your body and voice. As a performer and as a storyteller, your primary tools remain your body and your voice. Everyone has some experience getting attention from an audience. Then you can study further to make using your body and voice a learned art. Add to this the presence of Santa. When this is done with an eye towards appropriateness, it can be really effective.

Imagine Santa telling the story of the wolf in Little Red Riding Hood (or some type of Christmas variant). When Santa says something in falsetto with a bonnet tied under his nose, the little kids will be rolling in the aisles with laughter. Remember, Santa is toymaker-in-chief and must have a playful heart, to know what toys will work best.

Santa can be many characters, because when he performs as a character, the fact that he is Santa steps to the back for that period of time. Personal stories and stories you create yourself can also have voices, gestures, and characterizations.

Using costumes, props, and instruments. In the Little Red Riding Hood example, your "costume" might just be a bonnet. Or maybe you use a set of goofy reindeer horns. In some Santa-specific stories, one of the new items many Santas carrying is the "Magic Key" which allows Santa to get into places that don't have chimneys. If Santa lost the key or had it swiped, you could have the makings of story that fits nicely into the story you can tell. Instruments can be great fun, and music fits hand and glove into storytelling. For inspiration, look to the folk music and comedian communities.

How do I get started as a Storytelling Santa? First of all, think of yourself as a Storyteller. There are many storytelling organizations with events and festivals. Since Santa works with children so frequently, I would recommend trying some stories on some friendly groups, children of friends, or maybe someone's grandkids. Once you have a few practice audiences and stories under your belt, find a friend who knows something about performance. They can help you evaluate what does and does not work. Then practice some more.

How does this effect what I offer, and how do I pitch this to my clients? Before you offer it as an option, make certain you feel comfortable doing it. Have a variety of stories to offer and know exactly how long they run. Many people don't know what a storyteller does. "Oh, you're a Storyteller... So, you read books to kids, right?" I hear that comment from time to time. So you may need to explain what you do and give them a very brief synopsis, a couple of sentences should do. The main advantage that being a storytelling Santa gives you is content. You can add this to your list of performance options and delight audiences, and give longer performances for your clients.

A word about Storytelling Etiquette, some advice.

Make certain you do your best to avoid going over time.

Your audience comes first. Don't bore them and always leave them wanting more.

Try to make certain your story fits the right type of audience.

Don't duplicate stories you've heard from others, without getting permission first.

Watch out for copyrighted stories. If you make money doing something that a company owns, that could be a problem.

Do your best to always improve your art.

Help other storytellers when you can.

Your stories and storytelling have value. Don't undersell yourself.

Singing for Santas

This may be more familiar ground, since most Santas have lead people in "Rudolph the Red Nosed Reindeer," "Jingle Bells," and more. But if you want to raise it to another level, let's look at some options and concerns. First, be aware that people in today's culture are often uncomfortable when asked to sing, but kids usually don't have that problem. Children want to participate. Adults can be slow to start or some want to jump right in. In all cases, it usually can't hurt to ask the clients if this is agreeable to them. Then inquire which songs might be most appropriate. Overly religious songs might make some people feel awkward, while "Grandma got run over by a reindeer" might be just a bit too humorous for some crowds.

Handy Santa True Tip: I like to carry a batch of small jingle bells on bands. I hand one to an adult or teen that can help the kids stay on time and then demonstrate. "Everybody ready? *** Jingle Bells, ***Jingle Bells, and so on. The key is to stay high energy, and interactive, and very encouraging.

Do you have training as a singer? There are many ways to get training as a singer. You can join a barbershop quartet, a choir, or find a vocal coach. Or find a school that has music classes. Some organizations like Boy Scouts also encourage singing and are always looking for people to help. If you have friends who do karaoke, they can often point you in the right direction. Plus there are many resources online, including YouTube. Remember that when you perform, you want to make certain you stay on key, know your lyrics, and project at the right volume for the room (soft where appropriate, boisterous and ringing where needed). Before you start tackling seriously challenging songs like, "Oh Holy Night" in front of an audience, be sure that this is the right audience, and that you can do this song, perfectly on key, every time, and that you've had someone who is a trained singer give you the thumbs up before you take it on the road.

Do you have a repertoire? Songs are like stories. You need the right songs for the right audience. It's generally a good idea to have at least a few very popular and simple secular (non-religious) songs. Practice singing "Rudolph the Red Nosed Reindeer," "Jingle Bells," "Santa Claus is Coming to Town." If you have some songs in other languages, like "Feliz Navidad" or "Riu, Riu, Chiu," you will win big smiles from an audience that include people who speak that language natively (as long as you do it right).

Common Christmas carols often have some religious elements, which might be good for the right audience. "Silent Night," "Joy to the World," "Tannenbaum (O' Christmas Tree)," "Deck the Halls" are good examples. But if you are performing as Santa for an audience with a higher percentage of Jewish or Indian members, you may need to stick to the secular songs.

For the more sophisticated crowd, traditional Wassailing songs include, "Somerset Wassail," "Here we come a Wassailing," and "We Wish you a Merry Christmas" give you a great opportunity to talk about Christmas traditions of history. Likewise old carols such as the "Sussex Carol," "the Boars Head Carol," and songs like "Gaudete" will impress people who are really into their Christmas lore.

How good is your audience interaction? Use strong vocal projection to make sure everyone can hear you. Before you go on, have a friendly person stationed in the very back to give you a thumbs up or down. When people cannot see you or hear you, that's a real disappointment. But at the other extreme: Don't blast your audience. If you are going to be on microphone, take a class, practice working on microphone, and be very aware of where your speakers are. Remember that amplification does not make your singing voice better; it just makes it louder.

If you are leading a sing-along, you may want to provide some simple handouts that they can keep (coincidentally with your contact info). Not all people can sight-read music, so keep it simple. Remember: Do not charge for the handouts, especially if they contain copyrighted songs. Print the lyrics in larger type, especially if it's going to be outdoors.

The more you interact with your audience, the more they will support the song and join in. You can encourage good voices and enthusiastic people. You can lend your support to folks who are shy, by lowering your voice and joining with them in a non-aggressive manner.

Do you use instruments? Most Santas that play instruments tend to do it very well, and can sing as well. If you are bringing an instrument to a gig, make sure that it is tuned up as soon as you pull it out. It's even better when Santa has an assistant who can do the tuning for the right song and hand it to Santa when ready. Your goal as an instrument-playing Santa is to keep your fiddle time to an absolute minimum.

You likely won't be able play an instrument in gloves. If you are using electronics, the people who are working sound need to know in advance what you need. Also make sure your tuner, if you need one, has fresh batteries and is in working order before the gig. Carry everything you need—for example, if you play guitar, be sure that you have your extra picks, extra strings, Capo, and any other tools.

When there is a festively decorated music stand and instrument stand right out front, this tells folks what is going to happen. If you are performing outdoors, make certain you have sufficient light, and a way to hold any papers down. If you use other cards or aids, be sure there is a place to store them or access them. Also, remember that instruments and props need to be watched and cared for. You don't want someone to step on your five hundred dollar ukulele by accident, because you set it down to take a quick picture.

If you are bringing an instrument, try to find an assistant to take care of your gear and keep it safe from harm. Talk to the event coordinator beforehand, to have them provide a place where you can safely stow it. And learn to do an inventory, when you get ready to leave. If you are providing instruments: jingle bells, kazoos, or what have you, make them cheap, durable, and cleanable, if you intend to reuse them. Remember that little children, under the age of four, should not get jingle bells, due to choking. If you hand out instruments to your audience, hand them to the parents of small children (just to be on the safe side) and let them supervise.

Santas who can sing, tell stories, and play instruments, have a lot of options!

May your performing Santa be excellent, in demand, and may you get that highest of compliments.

"You are the REAL Santa!"

Robert Seutter, aka Santa True and also known as *True Thomas the Storyteller*, is a professional storyteller who has been storytelling for more than twenty-five years. He has helped create storytelling festivals, and was Director and Chief instigator for a non-profit organization (Dream Shapers) dedicated to promoting the folks arts. He is also a published author and a professional "Concierge" Santa, based in Thousand Oaks, CA. He can be reached for workshops, coaching, and performance training, as well as a myriad of storytelling personae, at: robertseutter@gmail.com, santa@santatrue.com, truethomas@sbcglobal.net, and his websites include: truethomas.com, santatrue.com, robertseutter.com, and on Facebook you can find True Thomas the Storyteller, Santa True, and Robert Seutter – Author. Telephone is 818-762-9075, and he's always glad to chat with his fellow performers and help where he can.

*This chapter has been reprinted with permission from Robert Seutter (Santa True), © 2015 TrueCo Publishing.

Santa Nana - Remembered

Gordon, I would love if you could include this "note from Santa Nana" in your next publication. :) *Santa Nana*

Mrs. Claus

Who feeds the reindeer all their hay?

Who wraps the gifts and packs the sleigh?

Who's helping Santa every day?

Mrs. Santa Claus

Who keeps his red suit looking nice?

Who does he turn to for advice?

Who gives the brownies all their spice?

Mrs. Santa Claus

She pitter-patters all around the workshop

The whole year long

Amid the happy clatter of the workshop

She sings a merry, merry Christmas song

Who reads the notes from girls and boys?

Turns in the order for their toys?

Fills every heart with wondrous joys?

Mrs. Santa Claus

Read more: Nat King Cole - Mrs. Santa Claus Lyrics | MetroLyrics

Santa Claus is one lucky fella. He has a wonderful life and a wonderful WIFE. What does Mrs. Claus do? Well, she can do EVERYTHING! Whether your "real life" wife plays Mrs. Claus with you, or you work with an independent performer, Mrs. Claus can greatly enhance a child's visit with Santa. If your wife is Mrs. Claus, the two of you will probably divide up the business elements according to each of your greatest strengths. Is she the businesswoman who keeps your calendar straight, your business cards stocked, and your web site up and running? Is she a twinkly performer, pulling an elf out of her hat and singing a rousing chorus of Blitzen's Boogie while jingling around the Christmas tree? Whatever the balance between you and Mrs. Claus, she can make the difference between a regular Santa visit and a spectacular one. A Mrs. Claus can often soothe a frightened child and buffer the transition of a child onto Santa's lap. A Mrs. Claus might calm the children down by reading them a story or two. Sometimes Mrs. Claus is the life of the party, and sometimes the two of you can collaborate your talents for a Christmas performance no one will ever forget. Mrs. Claus might put on a puppet show or take pictures. Mrs. Claus can hand out "giveaways," and Mrs. Claus can make sure you are the most handsome, fluffiest, stylish Santa, ever!

If you are lucky enough to have a Mrs. Claus by your side, you have the privilege of sharing the fun of the holidays with another. Mrs. Claus can benefit from performing-art schools and schools specifically for Santas, right along with you. Be a part of a local Santa group. Go to Santa gatherings across the country - - and expand your Santa knowledge to Europe and Asia.

Creativity counts! Currently, Mrs. Claus has a great deal of latitude on her costuming and talents. As a start, we may think of Mrs. Claus as being very, very nice, in Scandinavian clothing, having light-colored hair, twinkling eyes, and baking cookies. After that, she pretty much can create her own individual character - - but it should coordinate with her Santa. If he is wearing velvet and fur, she should be wearing velvet and fur. The reds in their costumes should match (or be complementary). The jewels on their hats can match. If he is in his workshop attire, she can be in her kitchen attire. After that, it's all up to your imagination. Before performing together, do a "character building" exercise so the two of you are on the same page. If your Santa is based on the Dutch immigrant model (Coca-Cola/Sundblom), imagine being the wife of a wealthy toymaker at the turn of the 19th Century, and what she might look like.

Of course, Santa and Mrs. Claus can appear on their own. When they do, the children may ask, "where is Santa?" or "where is Mrs. Claus?" And your answer is? Endless. At the workshop, in the kitchen (Santa likes to cook, too), with the reindeer, helping somewhere else. Make your stories fun, but within the known parameters of Santa. There is a North Pole. And in the North Pole there is a workshop. And in that North Pole there are elves. And there is a barn, and in that barn there are reindeer. And in the house there is a kitchen, and it that kitchen cookies are baked. There is a sleigh. And on Christmas Eve that sleigh flies around the world to deliver presents. Around that, there is lots of room for your personal stories about Santa and Mrs. Claus. Creating your own folklore is so much fun.

Remember that you are a role model for children. Santa and Mrs. Claus should represent a happily married couple who adore and support one another. Having good manners is always a plus. Santa should open the door for Mrs. Claus; Mrs. Claus might brush a crumb from Santa's beard and kiss him on the cheek. Christmas is about love. Hold hands. Say please and thank you. Always let your Santa hearts shine.

And while we are on the subject of shining, don't forget that sparkly, shiny jewelry and costumes delight children. Transform the ordinary into the extraordinary with every detail of your attire. Learn to use makeup. People are taking pictures that will be part of their family heritage albums forever. Appeal to all the senses - - ring bells and play music. The smell of cookies and cinnamon is always sweet. Make sure your entrance and your exit are something for everyone to remember. Most of all have fun. Have fun, and remember it's all about the children, and the child that lives deep within us.

Believe in the magic of Christmas.

Santa Nana

Personal Note:

My last chat with Nana was Jun 20th, 2016. We stayed in touch and compared notes back and forth for several weeks after I last saw her in person back in May. Both of us were fighting cancer at the time and Nana lost her battle July 9th, 2016. Santa Nana was a most wonderful, sharing person, passionate about her advocacy, and a leader in her field. Many miss her, as do I. — Gordon Bailey

Clown Squeak Gaff

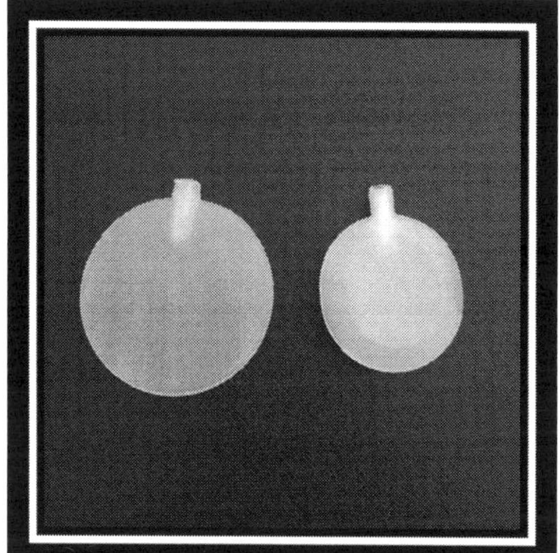

The gizmo(s) in this package create squeaks, whistles, chips, or "yips" when pressed or squeezed. In use the gimmick should be concealed and the movement required to squeeze it should either be hidden or lost in a larger motion.

For example: To make a sponge ball squeak the gimmick is held in the palm by curling 3 fingers around it while your thumb and forefinger squeeze the ball. This is not "palming"—3 fingers are naturally curled to keep them out of the way whenever you squeeze something, pick up something, poke something, push something, or even point at something. The motion of the hand hides the slight pressure needed to create the sound.

The secret of ventriloquism is that human hearing is basically non-directional. The noise you make will seem to come from anything that moves, is squeezed, pushed, or even merely looked at.

The best way for clowns and practical jokers to use this gaff is simply to hold it in the palm. Here are some ideas using the gaff in this way:

1. It is easy to hold gaff with 2 fingers while holding pen, lighter, or fork).
2. Squeak as you "flick your Bic."
3. In a restaurant push a fork into a steak and squeak. Say, "I said rare, not alive!"

4. In a restaurant tell people you are an actor just back from Hollywood where they gave you a good role (roll). (On the word "role" pick up a dinner roll and squeak it.

Following this you can do the bounce the roll off the floor gag. (Roll is thrown below table where it is secretly caught in other hand, foot is tapped on floor, hand below table tosses roll to hand above table. When timed right it appears you have bounced the roll off the floor. A "squeak" may be added as roll supposedly hits floor.)

5. "Squeal" as you take a drink. Say, "Well that really wet my whistle."
6. Press one of the spots on a playing card (squeak). Say, "You know what that was? That was a pipsqueak."
7. Squeak repeatedly as you wind your watch. Say, "Gotta get this oiled some day."
8. Press on a dinner plate, squeaking wildly. Say, "I've heard of squeaky clean, but this is ridiculous!"
9. If you or anyone says, "Am I a man or a mouse?" this is the perfect place for a squeak.
10. If someone swats at a fly or kills a bug, a well-timed squeak can be very startling.
11. Squeak when you press an elevator button or buttons on a vending machine.
12. If you see a picture of a girl, press her breast and squeak.
13. Paul Diamond contributed the following:
    a) Scratch your thigh (squeaking) and say, "I've got chirpies! It's a canarial disease... It's un-tweetable."
    b) Stamp foot along floorboard as though trying to squash a running cockroach. On the 3rd stamp,

squeal the gimmick and say, "That was a BIG one!"

c) Walk straight-legged, swinging one leg out in an arc and squeal. It looks and sounds like you've got a wooden leg with a rusty pivot.
d) Punch holes in a shoebox. Use gizmo to make "yipping" sounds. Ask people if they want to see your little dog. (Have a rubber hot dog in the box.)
e) Squeak gaffs are great to use with fur spring production animals or for mice finger puppets.
f) May be used as voice for any puppet or toy. You can even make a child's own toy start squeaking.

This gaff is great for clowns and magicians. "Squeak," "Squak," or "Squeal" when the water snake jumps out of the kid's hands, when the wand falls apart, when the flower droops, when the snake jumps out, or even when the flash paper flashes. For children's patties or shows!

1. Give kids the shivers when you ask them to reach into a bag or box (held too high for them to see into). Tell them there may be a snake in there. (If they withdraw their hand tell them there's no snake in there.) "There may be candy in there." (If you can tempt them to put their hand in the box) say "There may be a rat in there!" (Then squeak wildly!) This routine can also be used with change bags.
2. Sponge ball tricks or multiplying rabbits become much more entertaining to children when the balls squeak.
3. Do a 3 shell game with 3 sponge balls, one of which squeaks. Whenever someone picks up the ball they think squeaks say, "No, it's this one." (Pick up another ball and squeak.)

4. Pretend a child has swallowed your imaginary magic whistle. Every time you press his tummy the whistle blows.
5. Lightly squeeze a child's nose (squeak!). Have him squeeze your nose (no squeak). Have him squeeze his own nose (squeak!!). Kids believe it!
6. Take the noisemaker out of a small party horn. Have a puppet Mow the horn (squeak). Whenever you blow it you only get a hiss (and red in the face).
7. Cut the squeakers out of 3 rubber squeak toys (like the rubber mice you get at pet shops for cats to play with). Show that only one of the mice squeaks. Play a 3 shell game to find the one that squeaks.
8. Touch a child's hair (squeak). Say, "You must have washed your hair; it's squeaky clean," or "You must have rats in your hair—or at least mice!"
9. Press the buttons on a child's clothes and make them "chirp."
10. If you use a live mouse, guinea pig, hamster, bird, or rabbit in your act, make it squeak whenever the animal moves its head or sniffs the air. (Kids don't usually know what sounds these animals make.)
11. Touch the spots on a playing card (squeak). Say, "It makes sounds because it's a “playing” card. You know what makes it work? The pips squeak!" (Press one of the pips and squeak.)
12. In a magic production such as the square circle announce that you are going to produce a live mouse out of an empty box. (Act startled as a "squeak" comes from the "empty" box.) "Uh, from an empty..." (Squeak again. Stare into the box in mock anger.) This can go on as a running gag for some time. Pull a silk out of the box and act as if the mouse is trying to hold it. Using a cheap reel (Bill

Snatcher) or even a rubber band tied to one corner of the silk and the silk nearly just as it is out of the box and the mouse will apparently pull it back in. (Make wild squeaks and stare in box.) Put your hand in the box, let out a yelp, and pull your hand out quickly as though mouse has bitten you. (More squeaks.) Put a mousetrap in the box (don't actually set it, just pull the wire back so it will snap when you let it go). As the trap snaps, leave your hand in the box and do a "slow burn" (meanwhile pry the wire up so you can bring out the trap with your fingers caught in it). The mouse can meanwhile be squeaking away with glee! A live white mouse or fur mouse puppet can be produced as a finale.

13. A shorter version of the above can be done impromptu just by asking people if they want to see the mouse in your pocket, then squeaking as you try to get the mouse out. People who are afraid of mice will be sure you really have one and will jump straight up if you pull something out of your pocket and throw it at them.
14. Kids go crazy trying to make their "balloon heads" or "balloon animals" squeak by squeezing their nose or tail after they've seen you do it. Let several kids try it without success, then suddenly squeak when another kid tries it. (He'll be the most startled of all.) Ask him to explain how he did it (to the others who couldn't).
15. Squeak gaff is great for misdirection in magic. Make a ball or coin squeak when you're doing something sneaky with your other hand (such as loading a chop cup or sneaking another coin onto the table).

16. Pull a doll or toy with a squeaker in a cloth bag and have it answer questions by squeaking once for "yes" and twice for "no." (Use one of the methods of concealing the gaff.)
17. Act as though you're getting ready to sneeze violently (take rapid, short breaths). Frantically pull out a hanky, then make a tiny little squeak and return the hank (with gaff concealed) to your pocket.
18. Carry one or more of these with you always; you'll think of dozens of on-the-spot gags. Don't put it in a tight back pocket or you'll automatically squeak when you sit down or bend over!!
19. Chase an imaginary varmint through the grass, hitting at it with a cane or stick. Squeak at each blow. It is hilarious; try it!

Tapping, pressing, or squeezing the gaff with various amounts of force can make various sounds. By blocking the air with a finger and suddenly letting go you can get a high-pitched squeal like a mouse or bird.

By tapping the mouth of the gaff while squeezing you can get a bird trill. Squeezing the edges of the gaff can get another variation. Different gaffs can be purchased that have a higher pitch (mouse or bird) or lower pitch (small dog or animal "yipping").

At a restaurant, place 2 forks several inches apart and place a cocktail straw or toothpick horizontally between them. Pull the straw towards you, rubbing it on the tablecloth (and squeak). Say, "Most people know you can make a noise doing this." (A lie, of course.) Now move the forks closer together. "But most people don't know you can do this..." Pull just the end of the straw on the cloth in the narrow space between the forks (squeak). "That's called a narrow squeak."

(Hang around and watch people trying to make straws and toothpicks squeak on the tablecloth.)

Methods of Concealment:

1. Under your belt or waistband. Can be pressed with your arm or, if positioned just right, can be pressed by merely tightening your stomach muscles. (This method is undetectable.)
2. With cloth, straw, or net shoes it can be in the shoe controlled by your big toe.
3. Fastened between your knees inside your trousers you can squeak it by bringing your knees together.
4. Fastened under sleeve at elbow you can press it against body. Use one in each sleeve so you can always squeak the side away from spectator.
5. Fasten one on arm at the point your arm would naturally rest on the edge of a table when seated. (Press against table edge for squeak.
6. Drop one on floor as you sit down and control it with your foot.
7. Hang one down back of shirt. Squeaks when you lean back on chair.
8. Simply keep them in pockets and press pockets.
9. Hold against or tape to the back or bottom of box, bag or magic prop.
10. If in a chair that tips a bit put it under chair leg.
11. In the armpit (squeaks when you point at something). A little more difficult than the elbow method but great for people who wear short sleeves.)
12. May be hidden in a hanky or behind a book or any object you are carrying.

Gaffs may be fastened to body or clothes at strategic points by means of double-sided tape, adhesive tape or bandages. You can even tape one inside your tie! Another method is to make a little bag from nylon hose material and pin this inside your clothes at the desired spots.

Have fun... Dr. Doom

Reprinted with permission of MYSTERY CASTLE—Columbus, OH

People and Companies That Have Supported This Book

In most cases, my supporters are veteran Santas, or people who have been in the business of offering professional Christmas services and products for years. Please, patronize their businesses. ***Santa Gordon Bailey***, RBS

Santa Gordon's Resource Pages

NATIONWIDESANTAS.COM

We place Real Bearded Santas,
Designer Beard Santas & Mrs. Clauses
Home Visits & Corporate Events

We offer Background Checks & Liability Insurance
Check out our website for Membership information

Call Nationwide Santas today @ 888-449-7464
or email Gina@NationwideSantas.com

Shop
Santa Tom's
SANTAS
CLAUSET
(817) 938-5974
SantasClauset.org

- Santa Gloves
- Santa Leather Belts
- Hats and Caps
- Watches
- Rings
- Santa Shirts
- Brass Sleigh Bells
- Santa Belt Buckles
- Pins and Brooches
- Buttons
- Keys
- Santa Tees

and many, many more Santa items

TOYS FOR SANTA.COM
DESIGNED FOR SANTAS BY SANTA
QUALITY & VALUES
BUTTONS • BUCKLES • BELTS • MORE
ToysForSanta.com
Believe
BELIEVE PIN IN 18K GOLD PLATING
HOLLY LEAF 18K GP BUCKLE
TOYS FOR SANTA
YOUR ONLINE SANTA STORE
FOR BELTS, BUCKLES,
BUTTONS, PINS, ID CARDS,
RINGS AND MORE
WORLDWIDE SLEIGH
DRIVER'S LICENSE
License CU-DEC24
Height: 6'3"
Weight: Plump
Eyes: Twinkling
Beard: White
DOB: 03/25/0270
Class: Sleighmaster "A"
Issued to:
Fabled Santa Claus
1 Christmas Tree Lane
Santas Village, North Pole
Fabled Santa
INTL SANTA SLEIGH LICENSE
MASTER SLEIGH PILOT WING PIN
SANTA'S SPECIAL REINDEER BUTTON SET
TOYSFORSANTA.COM
QUALITY • VALUE • SERVICE • SELECTION

Planet Santa
www.planetsanta.com
Leather Belts
Santa Boots
Bells
Gloves
Wig & Beard Sets
Bells
Mrs. Claus
Vests
Makeup
Bags
Elves
Cooling Systems
We have thousands of Santa suits in stock

$25
WWW.PLANETSANTA.COM
COUPON CODE: SANTABUSINESS
SPEND $100 GET $25 OFF
Enter coupon code in coupon box at checkout. Cart will then subtract $25 from the total.
Must be used during one visit for the full amount. Cannot be partially used on multiple visits.

PIERRE'S
COSTUMES

Join our team for the upcoming Christmas Season!

Become part of an Amazing Team making Christmas Magical!

Live Video Conference with You, Santa and up to 4 other Locations!

Contact Susen Mesco with the Professional Santa Claus School for more information!

Ph: 303-665-8280

email: SantaClausSchool@comcast.net

WIZARDZ

Heirloom Furniture

Wooden Puzzle Thrones & More

Introducing a new line of portable Santa Benches, Thrones, Mr. & Mrs. Claus Chairs and a matching Head Elf Chair. Each handmade chair is constructed from ½" MDO-primed plywood ready for paint and upholstery.

Their specially designed interlocking parts, pack flat for easy transport, easily assembles in less than a minute without screws, bolts or hinges - just slip-fit the pieces together and they lock into place with a simple wooden key. Each chair is fun, fanciful, and strong, able to support 1,000+ pounds, and includes anti-tip bracing for rock-solid stability.

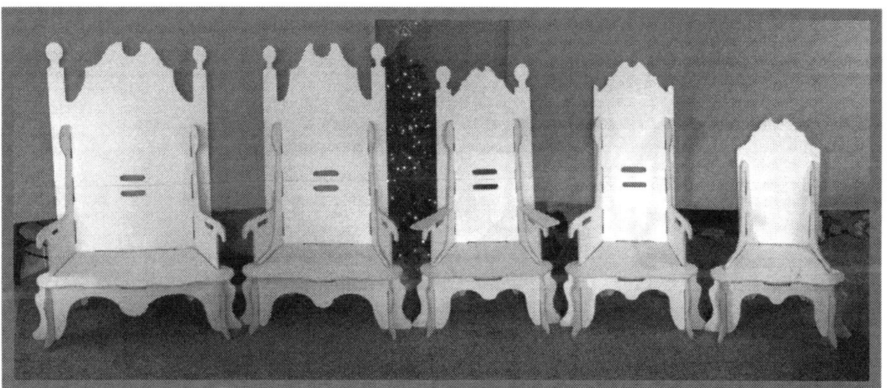

Model	Assembled Dimension	Shipping Dimensions	Weight	Price
Santa Bench	48"w X 63"h X 23"d	48"h X 36"w X 3"d	57 lbs.	$600.00
Santa Throne	36"w X 63"h X 23"d	48"h X 36"w X 3"d	47 lbs.	$550.00
Santa Chair	33"w X 59"h X 23"d	48"h X 24"w X 3"d	37 lbs.	$500.00
Mrs. Claus Chair	33"w X 59"h X 23"d	48"h X 24"w X 3"d	37 lbs.	$500.00
Head Elf Chair	34"w X 48"h X 23"d	48"h X 24"w X 3"d	27 lbs.	$350.00

Shipping & Handling: $125.00 – Each chair part is securely packed in form-fitting Styrofoam sheets for protection in transit.

VX Wizardz Heirloom Furniture • 801-979-5577

vxwizardz@gmail.com • www.vxwizardz.com

A mis

Jana & Mike [illegible]

818 968 4385

90123832R00080

Made in the USA
Columbia, SC
26 February 2018